Laced Bloodline

by

Kendra M. Harris

Laced Bloodline

Copyright © 2011 by Kendra M. Harris

All rights reserved. No part of this book may be reproduced or transmitted in any form or by any means without written permission of the author.

Wright Book Publishing books may be ordered through booksellers or by contacting:

Wright Book Publishing
www.WrightBookPublishing.com
email: info@wrightbookpublishing.com
1.877.266.5920

Because of the dynamic nature of the Internet, any Web addresses or links may have changed since publication and may no longer be valid.

ISBN 978-0-9822822-6-7

Story dedicated to my grandparents and their eldest daughter, Shirley M. Harris.

Also, my devotion is with my dearest sister-friend, Shelley Patrice Baham

Enduring the hardships of life
Sustaining the blows from the storm
Tuning to the silent messages with a special kind of listening
only given by God
Sheltering the wilderness
light through a dark path
self-indulgence ever so does repeat but it's grace,
guides our feet
Swallowed up by the worldly sharks
Taunted by the whispers which lark
our every dream desire to mark
We must lean on faith
refrain from biting Esu's bate
Mirages living
the mind's thresh
Walking in this cruel world
fooled by the tainted
tasty evils of refresh
But one drop, only one,
to remain in an array of dispense
letting the asphalt take away dignity and confidence
When the battle is fought
and the raging of the storm is calm
When the homeless is hovered and the bare covered
When the golden narrow path becomes grazed
with our prints and dents and sideward bends
When we've been good in spite of
and loved those enemies called friends
When your armor is weather
beaten and the victory is won
REJOICE! REJOICE!
For the Father says "Servant Well Done!"

Table of Contents

Chapter One 1
    The Gumbo Bowl 1

Chapter Two 5
    Adapting Growth 5

Chapter Three 9
    Journey 9

Chapter Four 29
    A New Destination 29

Chapter Five 37
    Revisited Dreams 37

Chapter Six 41
    Trey Bostich 41

Chapter Seven 51
    Valentin Castillo 51

Chapter Eight 63
    Bruce "Boogie" Thibodeaux 63

Chapter Nine 69

Tia Burgundi Bostich	69
Chapter Ten	**77**
Amina Thibodeaux	77
In My Journal	81
Chapter Eleven	**95**
The Gumbo Bowl	95
Chapter Twelve	**115**
Looking Back	115
Cybernetics & Paradoxes	127
The Author's Commentary	127
Simulated Lesson Plan	129
References	135

"Kendra Harris is New Orleans. She embodies its power to rise over suffering and celebrate the dance between life and death. This is a book that can be tasted and felt by deep body-mind-soul."

- *Bradford Keeney, Ph.D.*

Introduction

This book has been written, partially, as a non-linear subjective fiction (narrative prose) utilizing creative writing to bring forth academic discussion regarding metacommunication, cybernetics of cybernetics, and ways of relating to cultural complexities. You will encounter multiple circular stories. This includes a story told in a dream state and a story written as a journal entry that loops pragmatics to cultural communication (A *Pedagogy for Liberation, Paulo Friere, 1987*) which is discussed further in *Pragmatics of Human Communication A Study of Interaction Patterns, Pathologies, and Paradoxes* (1967) and *The Logic of Difference: A History of Race in Science and of Afro American Studies.* (2003). This book further explains what some view as a mystery about the perseverance of a people that has been rooted in a particular city by cybernetic ontology or generational lived experience.

This is good. I like the way the poetry flows in-between the storyline. It's rhythmic. It's jazzy. It reminds me of a second line, jumping spontaneously, but still in order, reminding of how the African mind moves."

Sunni Patterson,
Soul Singer, Poet Extraordinaire

Creative Narrative – Sociological Focus

New Orleans is an Africanized city that proves over and again that it is powered by generational cultural myths and realities that are, when presented to others, unspoken paradoxes to western modernity. With that said, there is a cultural clash within the United States that marginalizes its residents. American culture is a super absorption of ethnicities masked as one unified identity and powered by economical greed (social conformity).

The storyline, in this book, often leaps through time to uncover the past that is very much relative to the present and future ways of being and knowing. As years have passed, there are questions throughout the United States about the well state of the city of New Orleans and its residents. Questions are being posed regarding the progress of relationship, community, and industry. The answers that are given cannot be fully understood without lived experience or cultural exposure.

For example, there are new residents, teachers, and education administrators in particular who have traveled to New Orleans in an effort to assist in the rebuilding and unacknowledged reconstruction after Hurricane Katrina. This is truly accepted as a great deed. However, in most cases, ways of knowing are exceedingly dissimilar which, in turn, produces cultural clashes mainly in African American communities. This does not suggest a difference in educational criteria in its entirety. It does reveal a difference in lived understanding of requirements, "a discrepancy often misconstrued as a racially or economically-linked [deficiency] in achievement, rather than a mismatch in cultural expectations for linguistic [and academic] development." (*Cross-Cultural Semantic Acquisition: Evidence from over-extentions in child language*, Dr. Jennifer Bloomquist, 2003)

Creativity nourishes the growing mind. If it is incorporated into teaching and learning, creation and operation of systems, it can serve to spark a flame of understanding instead of using standard paradigms to manage a society of diverse people or multiple groups of uniquely diverse people in a society. A black and white, cut and dry blueprint for relating and knowing created by a supposed dominating cultural perspective will not be sufficient. It may be possible to say that cultural awareness, linguistic exchange, and creativity would, in fact, allow for a better response in the academic instruction and non-rebellious collaboration.

Speaking plainly, if we all acknowledged where we are in lived experience without judgment or direction leading to another's idea of where we ought to be, communication would be harmonious. In order to implement best practices for a community (any ideology, curriculum, program, infrastructure, etc.); a best practice would be to ask the people of the community. In this case, ask the people of the city.

Progress is slow, but forthcoming. If cultural differences and political voracity were recognized and addressed, in my opinion, the road to recovery, or even betterment, would be a swift journey.

Chapter One

The Gumbo Bowl

It was August, the hottest month in New Orleans. But instead of enjoying this hot summer month's end, I was making a decision that would soon change my life. August 28, 2005 fell on a Sunday. I was unable to sleep for worry of the hurricane that would soon destroy my home, soon destroy my life.

    After convincing those family members and friends to leave the city prior to Hurricane Katrina on the phone at 5:30 in the morning calling and warning, we were on the road. Packed with Lulu, Mama, and Valentin, my Cavalier was going on a journey. But before the start of this journey, my brother had to make a stop. And I was quite skeptical. He was only following me out of the city because I'd threatened him and made him transport Tia and Trey. But I followed him anyway, to the house of his girlfriend who was also riding in his car. Love, his girlfriend, had to make sure her dog, Fam was secured and had something to eat. And we were off.

    Time had zoomed by. I was frustrated because it took four hours of convincing and negotiating to get my family to pack something and leave. My convincing turned to screaming, crying, cussing and damn near fighting, but I knew their plan to go to the Superdome would not work out. It was a gut feeling. So we, Valentin, my children and I, stopped over to my mother's house before heading out to the highway for evacuation. This is when it happened. I became a little emotional and quite frustrated because I could not believe that they had not done anything in preparation for this evacuation. My brother was asleep on the floor in the living room and his girlfriend asleep on the sofa. My mother was sitting on her bed with the news station broadcasting – telling her to leave! My grandmother was sitting at the kitchen table unable to really get around and draining liquid from her back. Oh My God! I lost my mind. It's amazing what happens when you get a little crazy. "What are y'all doing?" My mother answered, "We're going to the Superdome if anything really happens." "Mama, New Orleans has never had a category 5 hurricane and I don't think the Superdome will be safe." After begging, pleading and crying, she started to put a few clothes in a bag. But my brother did not move. He was set on going to the Superdome. I was driving the old Cavalier and my two children, my boyfriend, my mother, my grandmother and our belongings could not all travel in that car. After all, I had to find room for my mother's dialysis machine. She has to dialyze every night.

    Ugly words were shouted and feelings were hurt and at last, my brother got up. So now here we were, gridlocked! We were on Airline Highway for hours and going nowhere. I was stressed and working to calm down but emotional because of what I went through to get these people to leave New Orleans. Cars were breaking down in the turtle slow traffic. Families were cramped into the back of pickups. We were out of gas. We stopped to get gas and got back into traffic, seemingly, in the same spot where we were before pulling into a gas station. "1 – 2 – 3" I have heard that counting gives enough time to mentally sustain. Every-one in the car, at this time, was antsy. Boogie, my brother, and I began entertaining one another as we drove. He would call me on my cell phone and tell jokes and I, in turn, would call him to make sure he was awake.

    The time had come once again, hours later, to refill the cars with gas. We seemed to be in the middle of nowhere. It was black like shut eyelids. Car lights were the only form of illumination. I called 911. "I am evacuating. I am running out of gas and I can't see anything; please help me?!" All of this poured from my mouth like gurgled blood as I became nervous. I was terrified! Becoming stranded, I thought to myself, would be horrendous because we were in the death of night surrounded by swamp land and wild creatures. "What do you see around you," the operator asked. Didn't I just tell this woman that I could not see a thing! I thought as I answered "M'am, I see nothing but a row of car lights behind me through the rear view mirror and red break lights from the cars ahead of me as we inch along. There are trees and road."

    I held the line until some sort of landmark was visible. The operator then led me to a gas station off of the main highway. It was easy to locate because it was the only source of light in that area. But Good Lawd, the line of cars to enter was extremely long. It was out of the station, two blocks down the road and continuing to lengthen. Horns were honking. Car lights were flashing. People were shouting obscenities out of the windows and roofs of their cars.

    The gas station's employees were frantically running down the road trying to calm all prospective customers. And there I sat in my car, still and quiet, taking deep breaths.

Chapter Two

Adapting Growth

The only way for me to remain in this present day, and not flip out as I would have back in the day, was to think of my newly discovered spiritual strength. Newly discovered only because over recent years I have tapped into what has always been there. My life has been so unbalanced and I, as a result, was a time bomb ready to go off. It started with the death of my father and the surgery to remove the brain tumor with which I was born. The operation came first.

I remember my daddy holding my hand and rubbing my head. I felt him and smelled him. I always knew he was near when I became delightfully overwhelmed with a whiff of smoky Egyptian Musk scented oil and sweet-smelling lilacs mixed with slight overtones of sawdust. But I was unconscious. I also remember is my aunt, my mother's sister.

I saw her when I was being transported to the operating room. Although I was heavily sedated, I saw her. Auntie Cheryl always spoke up on my behalf. She was hailing assistance, hysterically waving her hands and screaming because someone left me out in the hallway at Charity Hospital.

Although, Charity was a very good hospital – the best some might say, it wasn't the safest place in my family's opinion. Charity was a vacation home for the homeless schizophrenics and drug addicts. It was a familiar scene for the thugs and innocents that were stabbed, shot, or beaten bloody. It was the place that accepted unwed young mothers without insurance, like my mama, to give birth. I was born there as was the majority of black New Orleans. But Charity housed the best doctors. Teaching doctors, medical students from LSU (Louisiana State University) and Tulane University were all over the place.

For this reason, people, both white and black, traveled many miles to be treated. In most instances, Charity Hospital was all there was for the middle class and below. Dr. Ennis was the head doctor when I was there. The tumor was successfully removed, but my mama was told I would not be able to achieve highly. I would be average, if that. I had lost all function in the right side of my body. But I have always been carried by my ancestors and protected by God. They told me I will never live according to someone else's limitations.

My grandfather taught me to write again. He gave me inspiration. But I struggled. I carried a journal with me. Its pages were made for my thoughts, dreams, and ideas. I had always wanted to write a book. I began writing poetry.

It was therapy. Therapy allowed me to deal with the fact that my mother accepted me as handicapped and I just didn't fit in with the rest of the children at Joseph A. Craig Elementary School. I had become a much older soul. I had been equipped with "The Souls of Black Folk" and a perseverance that was undeniably made for a leader. I inhaled the wisdom that flowed from the pages of W. E. B. Dubois' literary work. Historical leaders such as Harriet Tubman and Marcus Garvey became magnetic forces for my rhythmic heart beat. They filled my cavity of a body like a filled tooth. It seemed to me that they lived in the neighborhood of my early days. The souls of my ancestors lived in Treme.

I was taught that dope is death in Treme. I was taught the significance of Congo Square where enslaved Africans bartered commodities and held reunions on Sundays in Treme. I was taught to open up just a little at my elementary school which was located in the heart of Treme. Treme is the oldest organized neighborhood in the country for housing both free and enslaved Africans. This neighborhood encompassed St. Augustine Catholic Church, a church founded by enslaved Africans. But I had also developed hatred for men in Treme, where my mother lived with her husband after moving out of the Iberville Housing Project. He beat me!

This violence was the beginning of my knowing how to hate and what face it should be given. I was angry. I fought boys (and girls) at school and in church. I did not talk to any man who spoke to me. That anger shifted by some means when surprisingly I became popular in junior high school and throughout high school. I was still reckless though. There were many prices to pay.

Chapter Three

Journey

Lulu rode shot gun. My grandmother, Lulu, had just dressed herself and called for a ride from the hospital on the Friday before the hurricane, and there was no way she was going to the Superdome, just now diagnosed with Ovarian Cancer, as long as I had breath in my body! She was ready though. "Ma big granbaby gon take car'o me." "Let's ride," she said. Back on that journey, on Airline Highway, we inched and stopped, and inched and stopped, and inched and then my brother hit me. He hit me hard enough to send me sliding into the truck in front of me. He fell asleep. Strength and patience is what I asked for at that time, guidance from my ancestors. "What would the ancestors do?" I remained calm. The driver of the small pick up got out of the truck too. People were yelling, "Move off the road" "Get outta da street!!" while blowing their horns and shouting the nastiest words, words so vulgar I couldn't hide my embarrassment for them.

"Lawd, help me?" My brother did not even get out, in fact, he began yelling at me to get back in the car. "C'mon!" he said. "Nothing is wrong with that truck!" "Man, we ain't got time for that!" I got in my car and drove away, with an aching back and bruised knee from the accident. I swear, with all the pinned up stress, if it wasn't for the look on my grandmother's face that said we are still family, it would have been a beating on Airline. Lulu saved him.

But we made it to the city of Baton Rouge. I needed to get to a hospital. Lulu's catheter, which was placed in her back to help drain the toxins because the tumor was too large to allow them to drain from her bladder, leaked. It leaked and bled on her clothes, in the car, on her spirit. It leaked.

But they were proud – "We'll make it!" "I don't want to go to no hospital." That was my mama, strapped with a catheter herself and in need to be dialyzed. I pulled up to the General Hospital and they were reluctant to take them but I would not take no for an answer. They were placed together in a triage room, both refusing to see a doctor.

I left with Valentin and my children. Boogie left too. Boogie and Love slept in the parking lot of the hospital and we rode a couple of miles back to the Waffle House. After eating, we slept in the parking lot across the street of a strip mall. The winds from Hurricane Katrina woke us. Signs fells, poles crashed, and the electric wires slammed together causing fire and sparks that terrified my children. Hell, it scared me too! But there we were, at least we weren't in New Orleans. I began to write in my journal...

"The Calinda is the dance I danced in my dream. It is the dance of the ancestors when they celebrated self and invited one another into relationships. I was always adorned with soft, flowing white linen that dragged behind as I stepped forward with a tall beautiful head wrap that shimmered. The air released a romantic scent that hypnotized all that inhaled and you took my hand, in my dream."

Summer days in New Orleans are filled with festivals and outdoor concerts. It's when I love New Orleans the most. In every love affair, the good has to be taken with the bad. And man, the heat and rain in July is bad. But I love it, nevertheless.

We were splashing through the grass watered by nature in Marconi Meadows to get to the stage because Doug E. Fresh was up next. As it began to rain again, the crowd scattered and we moved up closer. They all came out at once. Po' Righteous Teachers, Rob Base, A Tribe Called Quest, Doug E. Fresh, Slick Rick, MC Lyte, Big Daddy Kane; all I needed was Eric B. and Salt n' Pepper. Then, I would have felt as if I traveled back through time. I was high.

I floated on the sound waves and rode with the hip hop caravan to old school bliss. Those were my days. Those days held my bold vivaciousness. Those days held my "get out my way" attitude. In those days, I would have never let the love of my life keep on passing me by.

~~~~~~~~~~~~~~~~~~~~~~~~~~~

The winds tamed themselves just enough for me to gain the courage to drive back to the hospital. Boogie and Love were still in the car afraid to get out. Together, we went into the hospital expecting to have a whole heap of anger thrown at us. My mama and Lulu were right where we left them, in the triage room.

My mama explained to me the staff that had come on for the new day were very nasty. The head nurse told them to leave because no one had authorization to accept them. This was my argument: Too late! The overnight staff had already given my grandmother a place to clean up and my mother a place to dialyze. Were they going to put them out on the street? They both had insurance to be seen. Was it their fault they weren't given a room or even seen by a doctor? The paperwork was complete for admitting. I did it myself before leaving the previous night. Although, they were hesitant to see a doctor, they knew it was best.

Come to find out, these people never even stuck their head in the room or knocked. And the paperwork, I went to the desk to learn that the paperwork work had been shuffled around until they were no longer visible to the intake processors. We were not their usual patients, I found after looking around. The only people with faces like mine were the maintenance and kitchen employees.

This added more fuel to the fire. Fuel to show that I am a child of Africans tainted by the New World, child of Congo Square, pride given by the Africans who danced there on Sundays. I am blessed by my ancestors and I walk that way. But we remained without a place to go. I attempted once again to have Mama and Lulu stay at the hospital another night but this time they weren't having it at all.

I went to the playroom, in the hospital, with my four year old son, Trey. We spent a little time there. Then we visited the cafeteria, ate and returned. We even took a little nap in the playroom that was three rooms expanded into one because now there were more people without a place to go coming into the hospital. Later, we were up and ready to go.

Mama and Lulu were packed, dressed and at the door for the journey to continue. "We ain't staying here no more." But I explained to Lulu that we were sleeping in the car or on the ground and I just didn't think she should be exposed to those circumstances. She wasn't hearing it. My mother just stood and looked at me with the same look that frightened me as a child.

After the rain and wind stopped beating the tree limbs and buildings of the hospital, I drove. I drove with no direction. It was almost dark and the decision had come again, "Where do we sleep?" Well, I tried calling a distant cousin who lives in Baton Rouge, but her number had been changed and was not listed. I tried calling one of my mother's co-workers from Southern University at New Orleans who lived in Baton Rouge, but the answering machine picked up and I never received a call back from the messages I left. I tried the local shelters, but they were all full. So, I tried another parking lot.

This one was to an outpatient care facility operated by LSU. We parked toward the back corner of the private lot near the dumpster for fear that we would be told to vacate. I was tired. My brother had abandoned us. He drove to Alexandria by Love's family where there were 18 people in and out of a one bedroom apartment. So there we were in the parking lot. Tia, Trey, Valentin, Lulu, Mama, and me, of course. The children slept in the front seat. My mama and Lulu slept in the back seat. Valentin and I laid on the ground behind the car. It was my journal that magically held me in a mental calmness that cooled my soul, so I continued to write...

Hello lady, how are you? It was one of the men getting into an elevator as I headed home from my research class. They perspired as if they had just finished working out. They wore sweats and carried odd shaped duffle bags. The man who said hello wore a smile that shouted many more greetings than the "how are you" greeting heard. He wore smooth dark skin and a crown of free nearly natted hair. From that moment he watched me dance. From a distance, I danced and sang crescendo tones for the one who greeted me.

I included him in every decision made, but only if he knew. Or did he? His eyes carried the deepest glance that housed non-tangible intimacy. His stare burned the protective layer of skin that hid the sparkling shade of love that glistened all over me. "He knew," I often thought to myself. He knew!

We became friends. We shared stories from back in the day when hip hop was our life. We shared stories expressing what truly was the making of the person standing before me or the making of the person standing before him. We shared recipes, instruments, ideas and concerns. I shared my heart. And he knew! Did he?

~~~~~~~~~~~~~~~~~~~~~~~~

"We held hands and twirled around on sacred ground as we both inhaled the hypnotic aroma. The sweetest scent nestled the air arousing our wilds as we moved from holding hands to a full embrace. I saw Oshun as she moved her mirror toward me to shine my reflection within view. She then gave me a bouquet to remind me that I am just as charming. We swayed without a smile. I fell in love with you, in my dream."

Valentin and I slept on a blanket behind the car.

I always carried blankets in the car because when time permitted I would go to City Park. I loved it there. That was my beautiful. There should always be a place in your heart, a place you can go and find a beautiful mental relaxation haven. City Park was my beautiful.

There we were, asleep. Valentin said I even snored as loud as lions roared – I was tired. The morning came; it was time to get on the road again. I did not want the employees of this facility to report to work and find a family slumbering on the grounds. The people of Baton Rouge didn't seem to understand. There were jobs for them to report to, we didn't even have homes, never mind employment.

I knew the levees were broken back home because it was all that was on the radio, but I could not explain that to my grandmother. I turned the radio off whenever she was around. She wanted to go home. "Lulu we can't go home, they're not letting us go home because the water has covered the city." "What water chile," Lulu asked anxiously.

Lulu's house was in the hardest hit area, the Lower Ninth Ward. Her house, that she shared with my grandfather who had died two months before the hurricane, was one block from the Industrial Canal. Pawpaw was a carpenter. He built most of the interior for the neighborhood pre-school and the neighbor's homes. I remember when I was a little girl, Pawpaw and I walked up and down Deslonde St. visiting people. He would talk about jazz, and the war in which he fought, and black history. He told me what it was like when blacks didn't have much. But he taught me to be proud and determined. He said that's how he made it. He also built my aspirations to acquire an education. Pawpaw was one known for his penmanship, after all he had taught himself to read and write.

Pawpaw didn't get very much from his five years in elementary school. He had to help his grandmother raise his brother and sisters after Mariah, his mother passed away. But don't reckon with him, he was a very intelligent military man and self-sufficient black father. He was married for fifty-nine years before he died. Everyone loved him.

"Lulu, we can't go home."

And it happened early that Monday morning,
Blowing over the land of the Gulf Coast
Striking the flood gates at the levees
The Olde Creole Queen, as we know her,
was stripped of her gut
You took from her
the forever growing cultured souls
refined with all the Cajun spices
that seasoned her land
But she wants them back, the gut of her existence
She wants them back,
the culture bearers from the beginning of her time
The descendants of Bienville, Jeff Davis, Napoleon,
the city sublime
The descendants of the Thibodauxs,
Boudreauxs and Rouselles
playing jazz in ragtime
She wants them back
The descendants of the Bambara, Mandinka, Fulani, Wolof
and all other souls that sizzled, holding the blistering torch
as their psychological beings were attacked
She wants them back
The descendants of the ones who leaped in the air
dancing on free market Sunday at Congo Square,
She wants them back
"I am frail," she said, "trembling and bleeding,
and soaked from the muddy waters that filled
this bowl on that day.
I am squealing, weeping and still hissing
at the memories of my cultured souls being washed away
I am searching, hoping, and calling for the ones

*who are gone astray
I am sending peace to the ones who were troubled
without love
And leaning to a life of crime and dismay
I am shining immense lighting
for those who have lost their way
But pray. I say pray souls, to the African Powers*

*For they have the ultimate power
Reach up and get the power
Reach forward and receive the power
Reach back and give the power
Reach down, gain ancestral power
They've walked here before
Come back, my souls, run no more
Stand forcefully, run no more."*

    We continued to drive and I got lost, but what seemed to be a curse was actually a blessing. We sat on a dirt road with a flat tire. No one but Valentin saw that I was totally discouraged. He hugged me and said it's alright. He had me see where I had carried my family, out of harm's way. He reassured me that it would be just a matter of time before I find a place for Lulu and Mama. He was right.

Valentin put the doughnut spare on the car. We looked for a place to buy a tire, a used tire. We didn't have much money. Before we left New Orleans, Valentin had just come to my house from Shreveport, where he worked, to be with my children and me at the time of a potential category 4 disaster. He came back with a check to cash, but everything was closed. Before he arrived, we had a few dollars for gas to get on the road. But he was skeptical of the severity of the storm that was headed toward us and I was alone with Tia and Trey. As an African warrior, a provider, a strong family oriented black man in America, he felt he should be with us.

Valentin and I were preparing to deal with immigration before Katrina. He was born in Honduras. We had been together for six months and he was really assuming the responsibility which was dropped by my ex-husband. I loved him for that.

I stopped at a gas station to ask the location of the nearest tire shop. The cashier, who appeared to be amazed at how different my dialect was from hers, New Orleans drawl far from Standard English, I guess, pointed me in the direction of a shop down the street. Here, a Cajun man tried persistently to sell me a new tire. I explained to him that we were from New Orleans, and we hadn't much money and no place to go. He went beyond his duty for us.

"Oh, I got sixteen people by my house from

Nawlins rit now n' I know it can't be easy for yall outcher." He said, "I don't have a use tire to fit chou caw but I have one just a lil smaller than that size on yo caw. We are gonna rotate yo tires and put da smaller one on dee back at no charge – you should be all ite." This man went into his shop and had an employee call hotels around Zachary, LA to find shelter for my family. We had driven 15 miles. I didn't even know we had driven so far that we were in another city. There were no hotels available.

One of the employees called his church. This was the blessing. His church was preparing a shelter for those who had been displaced and wandering, like us. We went there. I felt a ton of pressure taking flight off of my shoulders. Now my mama and Lulu had a safe place to stay. But there was still one problem. Mama's dialysis machine was in the trunk of my brother's car and he was in Alexandria.

My journal spoke...

I'm surrounded by white smoke
Looks like clouds
And I see, ahead of me a man,
standing in a bright gleam
With open arms reaching out to me,
Proudly
And I, hoping to be drawn closer
and closer to him
But...suddenly the lights are beginning
to appear dim
But still he's reaching and waiting,
Patiently waiting with a flow'r
In his mouth, the stem
Finally we've met and petals fall
and the wind gently begins to blow

~~~~~~~~~~~~~~~~~~~~~~~~~~~

In the parking lot of my apartment complex, in Treme, where we all hung out, was the place I stood when I fell in love with hip hop. I remember looking over through the fence to see what was going on under the Claiborne Bridge. I remember smiling at the "Dope is Death" banner that blew in the wind as the cars sped on I-10 east. I saw the usual folks playing their boom boxes as they did a syncopated skip to the brass band melodies blasting from the speakers.

There were always people under the bridge, even as I fell asleep, their voices blared through my window. I heard cars pass with the stereos playing a song my mama loved so much. She had the album. I can still see it. The cover was sky blue. The color I see now when I think of hip hop. Rapper's Delight had a sound that was unique to me.

I listened to music by Odis Redding and Aretha Franklin; I guess you could say I've always had an old soul. I was influenced by the songs sung by Etta James and Billie Holiday. I fantasized about being there to place my eyes on Nina Simone when she sang of Mississippi. Goddamn, I must have been there! But now, I listened to a man say hip – hop - ahibby-ahibby ahibby, he was rocking.

What I heard was not test! He was rocking to the beat. I began to clothed myself with those words and I wanted to know more. Where did he come from? What is this music? I had heard nothing that carried the sort of beat that transformed the very beat of my heart. But from that point on, my heart played hip hop beats pumping out poetic lyrics to flow through my veins.

My friends and I started bringing our boom boxes outside to listen to this hip hop. We played baseball with sticks from broken window seals and shell rocks that posed as pavement in the parking lot. When a car window was hit, we all would break out running down the street but never leaving the music behind.

We ran down Governor Nicholls to see some crazy boys spin on their heads. It was a new dance. All lined up around a piece of linoleum lying on the ground, they clapped and jumped from side to side before they, unbelievably, spun at record speed on their backs, their shoulders, their knees, and their heads. It was incredible! And they played the same music, hip hop. What did they know that I didn't know?

They were older, maybe they had been to New York. New York was the place I found the music to come. Boogie Down Productions represented South Bronx. Heavy D represented "money earning Mount Vernon." I wanted to go there, but since I was still in elementary school, it was unlikely.

As the days passed, I carried a weight inside of me that was too heavy to ignore. I had to make a quest and since I was too young to leave New Orleans alone I had to make my own New York, where hip hop lived. Things were changing though. My mama, now, wanted me to catch the bus to my new school. She said with her going to work, she had no time to bring me to school. She said I was getting older and it was time for me to learn to get around the city.

My mama worked as hard as anybody trying to make ends meet. She couldn't keep a schedule that included transportation for me. So I learned to catch the public bus. The Sunday evening before I entered the seventh grade, she walked me to the bus stop and we waited for the St. Bernard bus to come. We boarded the bus and rode all of the way to my new school and home again. We didn't walk back home together though.

She walked home to get her car and followed the bus as she made me get back on the next bus to arrive, by myself. My mama drove behind the bus and took me home when I got off at the right stop. On the bus, all I could think of was how relieved I was that she never knew I was responsible for her cracked windshield. I never told her; it was just an itsy-bitsy crack anyway. It was a lesson learned, both the bus and the crack.

"Bruce, can you bring Mama's machine to Zachary?" "I don't know, I'ma see," is what he told me. I was furious. "Who told your ass to leave us anyway? You know our stuff is in your car!" My brother, Boogie, my mama's baby, never came. The church arranged for her to go to a hospital in Baton Rouge to learn to manually dialyze herself. They transported her and paid for the service. We were comforted. We also knew we could not stay here too long. We only had two weeks.

Eventually, Boogie and Love arrived in Zachary. He stayed overnight to see Lulu. Queen Lu is what they called her at the shelter. He slept on the floor next to her. Boogie never really displayed sentimental emotion but to know him is to know when he is hurting. He stays away when he is hurting. He is the youngest grandchild and I am the oldest of all of the grandchildren. The next day they went back to Alexandria. But the time had come for us to move on.

On the way to Texas, I met Boogie on the highway. We were off once again. We drove to Farmers Branch, Texas. Lulu's sisters were there. They had evacuated to my cousin's two bedroom apartment. When we arrived, there were 20 people, including us. One of my cousins rented an apartment in the same complex so that is where Valentin and I slept.

I learned that FEMA provided hotel rooms to evacuees. We went to the nearest hotel to apply. It was the Crowne Plaza on Midway Road in Addison, Texas. We were relieved. Later, I brought my mother to get a room. Silently, I hoped it wasn't near my room. I was exhausted and needed space. The rooms were next door to each other.

Later, we went back to get my brother, whose room in the hotel was across the hall. For our stay though, he managed to vanish even when he was in the hotel. His father showed up at Crowne Plaza hotel after being released from a Mississippi jail on a traffic ticket charge that should have been cleared. We hadn't seen him in awhile. But we, including me, were all glad to see him in Texas.

Valentin and I tried to remain high spirited even though we had lost everything. His clothes were there too. Without even seeing my home we knew there was no hope because the house was three blocks on the other side of the Industrial Canal, in the Upper Ninth Ward. The only thing we were not certain of is whether or not the house was still standing. On the radio, we heard of houses collapsing and people drowning. "What are we going to do?"

From then, I learned by doing, making mistakes most of the time, but doing, nonetheless. I became strong and independent as a junior high school student. On the bus, I learned all there was to know about hip hop. I learned names, and beats, and life stories of the artists. I learned, first hand, what the music, I so adored, was really expressing – survival. The music helped me to sharpen my memory. I began to remember, clearly, and understand the times in my young life when I felt pain. The music gave the mental place I lived a name, the jungle, and I was close to the edge. Hip Hop became my friend, and we shared everything. I began writing poetry to release that pain, like my friend advised. We were inseparable.

      To me, I was hip hop. I wore Salt n' Pepper earrings and had the flyest stacks in the city, even a stacked gheri curl. My jeans were artistically carved and my shoes were Addidis. If I had a problem, my friend was there, always, to comfort me. Hip Hop always knew what to say.

~~~~~~~~~~~~~~~~~~~~~~~~~~

      Summer days in New Orleans are filled with festivals and outdoor concerts. It's when I love New Orleans the most. In every love affair, the good has to be taken with the bad. And, man, the heat and rain in July is bad. But I love it, nevertheless. We were splashing through the grass watered by nature in Marconi Meadows to get to the stage because Doug E. Fresh was up next. As it began to rain again, the crowd scattered and we moved up closer. They all came out at once. Doug E. Fresh, Slick Rick, Big Daddy Kane, all I needed was Eric B. and Salt n' Pepper and I would have felt as if I traveled back through time. I was high. I floated on the sound waves and rode with the hip hop caravan to old school bliss.

~~~~~~~~~~~~~~~~~~~~~~~~~~

      As I sat in the class, with worry of the content held by the upcoming midterm exam, I listened to a peculiar sound that traveled from quite a distance in the building. Although slightly muffled, it was too clear to be someone's radio. I found relaxation in that *rhythmic sound. It was drumming.*

I was able to hear every naked palm slap the drum, making a honey hollow noise, and able to hear the quick tongued fingertips as they counter created a melody for an African journey. Soon, I was fully submerged in this melody, forgetting the anxiety carried as my professor lectured. I was no longer in my physical, for I had embarked upon a crowded journey of serenity.

The other students started to move to their perspective places when the class was over. Their movement had taken me away from my meditating state and anxiety had taken over once again. I fastened my pace as I gathered my notebook and pen, text book and book bag, to run to the elevators in hopes of finding the music that captivated my mind from hostility and brought an overlapping feeling of tranquility.

Finally, waiting for what seemed to have been a life time, the doors opened. Hello lady, how are you? It was one of the men getting off of the elevator as I, after changing my mind about boarding the elevator, headed home from my research class, pretending I was walking pass the elevators. They perspired as if they had just finished working out. They wore sweats and carried odd shaped duffle bags.

The man who said hello wore a smile that shouted many more greetings than the "how are you" greeting heard. He wore smooth dark skin and a crown of free nearly natted hair. Oh, I thought to myself, he is beautiful! Overwhelmingly, I ran toward my car, mentally. It seemed as if my feet just didn't move swiftly enough to get me out of such an awkward spot. This man began to walk with me. "Hello," he said again, wearing the brightest smile I had ever seen on a man's face. "Hi," I replied, looking at my Addidis. We began to exchange words that were small in spoken word but huge in spirit soon becoming best friends in a word. He walked me to my car taking the keys from my hand.

Mystery leaned over to unlock the door and, displaying a character that smelled of truth, he opened the door wishing me a warm goodnight and welcoming a tomorrow's hello.

~~~~~~~~~~~~~~~~~~~~~~~~~~~

I found an apartment in Addison, after being turned down twice because of my credit score. What a time to refuse a place to accommodate those displaced. My credit had been ruined due to my divorce. I had money, and I was educated. I paid a mortgage in New Orleans. But I was asked, even with the information on the application, if my prior governmental housing assistance and welfare were active. What the fuck!?

It seems that everyone outside of New Orleans have the impression that the residents of my city are poor, ignorant bastards. We were talked to as if we were idiots. Everyone I spoke with complained of the same. Racial inequalities were soaring through the air of the south. The discrimination that lived dormant was washed up and exposed as Katrina saturated southern soil. The, seemingly, true definition of the American Way was bare.

Look at me
Not with just your eyes
See the inner me, deep down within me
Know who I am, not who I could be

Laced Bloodline

Listen to me
Not with just your ears
Hear the sound I make so dear
Hear my laugh, my cry, my scream of fear
Know the sound that comes from me,
not what should be
Touch me
Not with just your hands
Feel my heartbeat
Know where I stand
Feel my joy, feel that I am human
Know that I am different in the sun and the rain
Know that crying and sighing,
loving and laughing I can
Smell me
Not with just a sniff
Know that my scent can be pleasant
or it can be stiff
Know that my scent can last forever
or it can breeze through swift
Know my natural scent comes from me - only me
Taste me
Not with just your buds
Feel the sensation, the bitter floods
See I am different just with a lick so
be careful of the flavor you pick
Know me
As me
For me
Accept me
Love me
Know I am me
Not who I could be
Not who I should be
To know me is to:
See me

To listen to me
To feel me
To smell me
To taste me
Before you judge me
First, I ask that you simply know me

Chapter Four

A New Destination

We lived in a two bedroom apartment. Amina and her mama shared an apartment with the same floor plan as ours. We inhaled, then exhaled. Relief. Lulu lived nowhere but New Orleans in all of her seventy-eight years. She liked the apartment. An apartment that was just an apartment to me was elaborate to my grandmother.

She was becoming very ill but still refusing treatment. I watched her. She was dying. But she was happy in that apartment. We laughed and danced and basically carried on as if we were down in New Orleans. It was the way for us. "Forget your sorrow and dance. Forget your trouble and dance," Bob Marley said that.   Auntie Cheryl visited us for Thanksgiving. She was there, also to see her mama and help my mama take care her. She came from Plaquemine, LA. That is where she evacuated. Oh! I was happy to see her. She is my favorite aunt. She was my Big Momma. I loved her so.

We played cards – she was the one who taught me to play Spades at age 9 and had been my partner ever since. We talked, ate, and laughed. Soon it was time for her to leave. "I'll be back for Christmas and I want one of them!" She was talking about a wooden incense box with picturesque motifs carved into the wood.

I had begun to make jewelry and sell oils, African art and artifacts in Texas while I sat bored to tears and longing for home. I was away from all that was familiar.

I searched for employment and although qualified, over qualified for some positions, I was not employed because I was from New Orleans. Employers often thought of the possibilities of New Orleans residents returning home and others just flat out refuse to hire.

She wanted an incense box. Auntie Cheryl never made it back to Texas. She was getting dressed one evening in Plaquemine to go to the casino with her new friends. She was going to the casino with her friends that had provided her a place to live. These were friends that were, in numbered years, older than her but called her Ms. Cheryl for her wisdom. She died. She had a stroke/aneurysm.

The doctors said she became brain dead in a short period of time. It drove me crazy not to be able to get to her. She was always there for me. Two weeks before Christmas, my family traveled to New Orleans to bury her. My cousins, Auntie Cheryl's children, could not be alone at this time. How are they going to accept their mother's death? Pressure had weighed in on everybody.

Back in Texas, Lulu had a seizure. My mother was afraid to tell me - but my grandmother had a seizure. We could not take her to New Orleans because she had become so weak. She had a seizure provoked by anxiety while we were gone.

I escaped to the pages that held my serenity.

During my drive home, I continued to smell that fragrance he wore. It was musky and sweaty but sensual scent no one could probably pull off but him. I wondered about his life. Was he a drummer only for

Laced Bloodline

the class that took in two floors above mine? Or, was he a professional traveling drummer who carried with him this scent on his African journey of serenity? Was he the King for whom I waited? What would he be going home to face tonight? I felt as if I was a silly school girl handing over a note that read –

DO YOU LIKE ME?   YES   NO   MAYBE

Or sending my mystery love school girl poetry like:

When I first met you I knew you were a flirt
Although I fell in love with you
I knew I would get hurt
I tried to tie you down to me only one
Trying to do something no one's ever done
Now you want our love to end and I try not to cry
Trying so very hard to learn
to kiss your lips good-bye
With my sorrow and tears, I'll always be there
Trying to find a love, one I don't have to share

I had begun to finish this love affair before it even started. I guess that is what I had been accustomed to in my life. There were never good things for me.

~~~~~~~~~~~~~~~~~~~~~~~~~~~~

His eyes carried the deepest glance that housed non-tangible intimacy. His stare burned the protective layer of skin that hid the sparkling shade of love that glistened all over me. "He knew," I often thought to myself. He knew!
We shared stories from back in the day when hip hop was our life. We shared stories expressing

Kendra M. Harris

what truly was the making of the person standing before me or the making of the person standing before him. We shared recipes, instruments, ideas and concerns. I shared my heart. And he knew! I believe he knew of all the guarded love I detained.

It was amazing how I expected this man to know what was inside of me. After all, he was just learning me. I was learning him but absorbed more of his soul with each communicable moment. I wanted him to know my wounds. I wanted him to know my insecurities. I wanted him to know my heart; the cut out in my heart had been measured and tailored for him. He is in my dreams.

~~~~~~~~~~~~~~~~~~~~~~~~

"No, I'm not doing that again." "I'm done with trying to have a happily ever after love story. It doesn't work for me," Tiye said as she sat throwing lumps of hardened dirt onto the pavement watching it crack with every impact. "I won't be telling the story of my change in relationships – how some mother neglected to embrace her son and now he's grown with overly affectionate issues or how society has pounced on some brother and left a docile man as a shell of anger waiting to explode soon unable to utilize his own judgment."

"It's not like that!" "In your life, make sure the man you chose has passion for something in his life other than you and, then, he will know how to love you," said Kolunde as he held Tiye's grimy hand, tilting his head around the edge of her face to make eye contact. "You have to be wise enough to see his soul, Tiye."

Laced Bloodline

"Anyway, you going to Michigan next week? I was hoping you could stop by my cousin's house to check on him. They say he's not doing well but I need to see him; I'll send your eyes." Tiye changed the subject of conversation to avoid looking into Kolunde's deep brown stare that told a story from the ancestors with each momentary look. She stood and brushed the grass from her ankle length dress which covered her naked body as she waited for his answer.

Yes, I am going. Give me his address; I need to talk to that brother anyway." "I haven't seen him since he moved up there. Cancer, huh?! Yeah, we need to wrap on some spiritual healing – He'll be alright!" Tiye hugged Kolunde as she said goodnight. "It's 2:00 in the morning" she realized as they sat underneath an oak tree in City Park near the carousal. I guess I'll go home and get some sleep. You get some sleep too and I'll talk to you tomorrow."

The day before my thirtieth birthday, my mama had a series of seizures. She had a stroke and a succession of seizures. The doctors told me to call my family because she was not going to make it. I am trying to forget the pain from those memories of mama in a coma and just one year later, Lulu had a seizure.

"I can't do this! I can't take no more!" But life assured me that we all have to endure in order to come out on the brighter side. And besides, I needed to be strong for my mother. She had just lost her father and sister. She is now losing her mother.

Well, Lulu passed away two days into the New Year. She came with us into the year 2006. Two weeks after burying my aunt, my family and I were back to New Orleans to bury my grandmother. I really can't take it no more.

Tia and Trey attend Holy Ghost Catholic

Kendra M. Harris

Elementary School in New Orleans. They have never before attended a catholic school. Trey was preschool age but he attended an independent African rooted school during his early years prior to the storm.

I had never paid tuition for my daughter to go to school. She attended a chartered school before the hurricane. The International School of Louisiana prepared her for our Texas experience. We were in a Hispanic community. With her Spanish curriculum, she knew how to communicate effectively. It even came in handy for me at times when I needed to communicate with someone who spoke too fast for me to understand. It came in handy when she had to say goodbye to her friends because we were going back to New Orleans. I couldn't take any more of being away from my home.

Chapter Five

Revisited Dreams

We, my children, Valentin and I, live in the Marriott Hotel now. I am in graduate school at Southern University @ New Orleans. The flame that ensue my determination to complete my studies must never dwindle. I will succeed because I refuse to limit myself. Earning a doctorate degree has always been a goal that will be accomplished for myself and for Shelley Patrice Baham.

      For as long as I can remember, Shelley was my very best friend in the world; she died of cancer in November 2003. I became numb. I began thinking that I had lost the only person in the world that understood me and still genuinely loved me.

Are you the soul who calls
out for companionship?
Are you the one who watches the sparkle
of the stars at night?
the one that implore some form of salvation
I know you, companionless one
the lonely soul without a friend
Your life is filled with many doleful moments,
your days - melancholy actions,
never having anything of significance to do
I know what you stand for
You're so lonely and so confused
Why are you so mysterious, such a nebbish being?
Why are you so full of anxiety?
You see in the mirror a nobody
who's going nowhere so why try?

Nobody understands you,
nobody except me
I'm just like you

We were to go back to school together but her dreams were cut short so they will live through my accomplishments. I will succeed for her. Also at present, I am trying to figure out the best way to rebuild my house which was completely destroyed by Hurricane Katrina. Now that my mortgage is paid, I have accomplished one of my life's goals. That goal is holding ownership of my home, escaping the burdensome cloud that hangs over ones head when lien holders are involved. It was a blessing from God delivered by Katrina.

Although the insurance companies have been close to invisible I know, somehow, I will figure out a way to repair my home. Many times I feel like we're alone – apart from the United States Government. Yes, New Orleans is rebuilding, but not really in my neighborhood. We are trying to get things together ourselves aside from the assistance provided by FEMA for rental assistance or the FEMA "shut up, you nuisance" money. I was taught to survive. We will succeed.

This is a story bearing similarities to most people's strife and victories that occur in their lives when dealing with pain, losses, and determination. There are few people to share the heartbreaking details outside of therapy sessions or support groups. My grandfather told me that clear expression comes through writing. The name Karasi Monet Burgundi (Bur-gun-di) carries a legacy given by Walter Burgundi, Sr. I will succeed because it never occurs to me to do otherwise. Pawpaw taught me that.

It was long ago...

*I have almost forgotten my dream
But it was there,
then, in front of me
Bright like the sun
And then a wall 'rose
'Rose slowly
Between me and my dream
'Rose slowly
Hiding the light of my dream
'Rose slowly,
Until it touched the sky
The wall shadowed me
I lie in the shadow
no longer the light before me
Above me
Only the thick wall,
the shadow
My hands!
My dark hands!
Break through the wall
Find my dream
Shatter this deathlike dusk
Break this shadow into a thousand rays of sunbeams
To illuminate my dream*

Chapter Six

Trey Bostich

Father said, there were leaders
who gave up life for the cause –
people to stand all wars
But they stopped breathing
"Keep thy heart with all diligence;
for out of it are the issues of life"
But without it what makes life for me
I hear tranquil breezes, yet murmured clatter
and I feel your withdrawal, mama
Father said, I am his and you are never to misguide me
but already I am experiencing growing pains,
seeing stains of evil through your skin
Been swallowing poisons as every sound wave
hits your eardrum
From this confusion, mama, I ask, what's going on?
I feel your touch which teaches the importance of
libation
and smile at your soothing lullabies by wise men
and it makes me know love is there
But I know not where, mama
I hear about manifest destiny and with Father,
I have met the Freedom Riders and Oretha Haley
I listened to Biko tell of apartheid,
listened to Mr. King tell of the stride
to the statue of Lincoln while drinking impressionable
juice
Choking when I saw the horrendous scars of hatred
on Emmit's face
The fast paced beat of my heart scares me
But Mother Tubman cuddles me

*and says it's alright black child
for we have made a way
Now I am almost here and Father whispers in my ear –
"No weapon formed against you shall prosper"
But there are no leaders just "up until the battle"
marchers
because the diehard leaders have stopped breathing
What am I to do – There's not even an education
advocacy, remembering Mrs. Bethune's Institute and
Mrs.Lucy Foster's longevity
What will I become?
Father said, "A powerful leader in my name, son,
until the day you stop breathing!"*

    My mommy woke me up extra early, I think. She tipped toed pass my door like she always does; she was trying not to wake me but it doesn't matter. I get up when she goes by.

    I saw her walking with clothes in her arms and mumbling to herself. When she's like this I know it's something grave happening or going to happen. The last time she mumbled to herself, my daddy had married another woman. I thought she was going to kill him. She thought she was going to kill him. My daddy lived in our house. We were a family. They were back together to mend the family that already existed in my eyes. He moved back in and they looked happy.

    I know Mommy was happy because she felt there was space left to proceed with the family she cherished so dearly. She wanted to forget the day she threatened Daddy if he didn't sign the divorce papers. My daddy would play with us, me and my sister. And we were happy too. But he married another woman and we didn't know. Daddy had two lives for a while…well until my mommy found out. My mommy also found out that he was sleeping around with other women. I don't exactly know what that means, but I know my daddy should have only gone nite-nite with my mommy because he was in trouble.

Before I was born, my mommy said her life had become filled with purpose. She and my sister had gotten married to my daddy. Daddy asked her for a son and my mommy said she hesitated to oblige because my sister's father had hurt her. She said she was afraid to become a mommy again. But she loved Daddy and took full position as his wife.

She thought, "My husband has asked for a child and I will please him." I was born in November of 2001. Mommy had become very ill toward the end of her pregnancy. She said I was too heavy for her pelvic bone – whatever that is. But finally the time had come. I was a healthy baby boy weighing 8 pounds and 2 ounces. She was happy and sad. She was sad, because I was born blue and purple. I had swallowed blood and could not breathe when I came down the birth canal. I don't think I was ready the first time down so I traveled back.

Mommy couldn't talk. She said she was in too much pain to inform the nurse, who was about two feet away. She and the doctor were watching the night time sitcoms on the delivery room's television set. In her mind, though, she yelled repetitively and very loudly, "My baby is coming!" But I fought to stay in this world, remembering the soothing touch through mommy's skin and her muttered melodic voice as she whispered African proverbs. I would listen to her tell me things like "It is easy to defeat people who do not kindle the fire for themselves" or "If God breaks your leg He will teach you how to limp so always have faith that you will endure, young King." I believed every word.

My parents argued all of the time about my

daddy never being home. He worked offshore and stayed at work months at a time. When he came home, he went by his friends. My mommy would scream bad words at him. She started to believe my daddy had a problem with her because she was American and he was Honduran. Sometimes Daddy would hug her as she cried holding me in her arms. He told her that those things she believed to be true were not.

She wanted to know the reason he drank so much, after all she worked hard to be the best wife she could be for him. But mommy was there before he started working offshore. She said she didn't really know my daddy anymore. My daddy had his own demons. He also had many obstacles in his life that he allowed to block his path so he remained in one place. Mommy just couldn't make him face the obstacles or the demons.

Because he stayed away on the water for so long, mommy began to accept the untruth of her being single. She dated other men. There was a man who would come to see her, but he only visited us for short periods of time. Mommy said he made her feel special. He bought flowers for her and toys for me and my sister. He even brought breakfast, lunch and/or dinner when mommy didn't move from the bed because she was so sad. Mommy said he was a virtuous friend, but in her heart she realized the likeliness of her accepting another man's love. At that time to her, her marriage had failed so she divorced my daddy.

Tall, deep chocolate brown skin, bald,
large hands, strong, muscular build,
wise, gentle man – I fell in love with him
He is my love
never made music;
I didn't want to accept love

until one year…
Sweaty passion
Sticky love muscles
Soft tongue caresses sang crescendo tones
After the long time winds had blown
I wondered what did I do
I really did love him.
I praised his magisterial presence.
I longed for the wisdom words that dripped
from his tongue
as we mentally sat on the shores of the
Niger River Delta
and listened to the ancestors sing
My skin dampened at his every minuscule touch
but time held too much
when he revealed his secret
Time held too much when I, too,
had the same new secret
Two men – I loved them both
for different reasons
and if combining them was an option,
I would have the perfect husband
but what about him?
Will his wife understand this extended relationship
on the outer surface of matrimony?
That lady's husband forever lingers around me
That lady's husband
Tall, deep chocolate brown skin, bald,
large hands, strong, muscular build,
wise, gentle man – I fell in love with him
He is my love
Twilight night shade of skin, broad shoulders,
locked lengthy hair, rough
man's man, beautiful spirited man
I fell in love with him because…
He was my foundation, my support,

a King that cherished my soul
I felt his warm cares. I seized his nourishment.
I tasted his love in the core of my being.
I am safe. And time held too much
when I married him..

    Tara lived in New York. Nelson was introduced to her by one of his friends. He drove to New York one evening after dropping me and my sister off at my mommy's job. He told my mommy he would be home after the weekend was over. He said that he was going to Texas with his friends to look for a truck to purchase.

    Tara was Honduran and Nelson Bostich, my daddy, didn't know her from their home country, but she was from the same village, Truinfo de la Cruz. She was younger than my mommy. Mommy always called her "lil girl." But that was the next year when daddy got in trouble. Daddy was in trouble when my mommy found out that he had married Tara in New York.

    He married her after he was stabbed in the abdomen believing it was my mommy's fault. He was stabbed by a man in a Latin club who had danced with Mommy. Mommy said he always asked her to dance, that man. I think he liked her, but my mommy just liked to dance and he was a good dancer. My daddy didn't want any man around my mommy. He would often fight with men that attempted to court her. All of the men who stood and admired mommy in those Latin clubs were apprehensive to dance with her for that reason so she danced alone most of the time. She never cared. She said she danced to cleanse her soul. The sweat that trickled from her brow was little bulbs of negative energy being expelled from her sanguine spirit.

    But my daddy was jealous of any man who could possibly take away from him the person who loved him the most in his entire life. He stalked her! He even burglarized our home. It was Mommy's thirtieth birthday. She had some friends from out of town over to celebrate her years on earth. Nelson was told that they went out to a club and that Mommy was with one man in particular. This was amusing to my mommy being that she hadn't seen Nelson for five days – he never even called to wish her a happy birthday. But he shattered the window to her bedroom early Sunday morning to drag one of Mommy's house guests out of the house on his back. Mommy fought to move from that place in her life that held her in mental bondage. She had to permit her heart love again but I, a growing baby boy, required a father.

Keep your head to the sky…

Is what I hear
Just leave me be with the mirrored reality
staring in my face
Sqreaching-chanting, I wish it was over,
I wish it was over - is my soul,
the voice of my spirit
is the hidden reality
Just leave me alone by myself to awake
what is real
to release the dark chains
boomerangs of depression
to sleep and find fantasy
because I've never been happy
Just leave me a loan to buy the room furniture
for livin',
the kitchen eating table,
the food to nourish and call this home
just leave me alone
My friends, so-called friends, family,
enemies feeding off of my character

'cause you say I'm strong
because you're like thorns in my fingers,
splinters in my nose
blood of the innocent on the hanging tree
you make me flee from your vibes
because dodging every blow is what you see
but you don't see me bleeding to death

Keep your head to the sky

Just leave me a man, a masculine man,
a daddy, my daughter's daddy, my son's daddy
to love and nurture their seed
…to protect their own
I wish it was over so life could just leave me alone

To find my soul on Common Train

To feel my pulse in rhythm
To live the music of the congo
I hear it - it talks to me - it tells me my destiny
To taste, drip by drip, on my tongue
The sauce of the drum
The words so righteous,
The universe just moves me
So I dance
To heal all wounds
To soothe the scars in my womb
To conjure up praise for hours - never cease –
it tells my story of peace
I sing to harmonize
with the harmony the strings give
To deal with the scantiness of union
Protecting against ruins of the sparkling diamonds
in my eyes

To forgo hatred
The musico tells me to live for me
and the symphony explodes with tunes only
I hear
So I dance
To move
To get up and move
To get up and move from the seat where X seems to mark
the spot put aside for my life, at boarding
Watching Common Train, with blooded brakes,
coming to take away my LIVELY self
So I stand on the tracks, mentally
Dancing, but paralyzed
blind, deaf, standing
on the tracks, STILL,
standing, dancing on the tracks
unable to get on that train
Beat the congo, stroke the strings
Sing me a song
To move me - it's coming - that train
To mutilate my dreams
To take away my soul - sing me a song –
stroke the strings –
beat the congo
It's coming - that train
Play the music - to move me - so that I can move
Play the music, so I can dance
So I dance to save my life
cause my soul was never on Common Train

    I slept next to Lulu in the shelter. Mr. Valentin would cover me with the blankets that were donated by the church. He would whisper tales about strong African men in my ear as I fell asleep. When I woke up, he was there. "Let's go to the bathroom, my boy. We need to get cleaned up." I quickly jumped up and ran behind him. I like him. He took me for walks along the dirt road in Zachery, Louisiana.

He took me to the church's basketball court and taught me to bounce the ball and shoot. He took me – in his arms to hide me from the present reality. I was happy traveling with my family on this vacation.

Chapter Seven

Valentin Castillo

There's a place where the air smells of pine
and silence sings pure jazz
To sit along the banks would be soul relaxing
I want to live there
Where living is simple, far away from the rat race
Living is just that there
I want to go
Let down my hair
...and breathe

      I was successful this time. Man, I've been to that border three times already! The boss man told me never come back to the shop. He wasn't paying me enough to feed a lab rat anyway. The customers knew I was the best mechanic in Le Ceiba so those side jobs were easy to come by. There was no way I could provide a way for customers out to my house though, from the city of Le Ceiba to a Garifuna village on the coast, and besides all of the equipment I needed was at the shop.

      On the bus, as I traveled home to Truinfo, I could not control the impulse urges that poked at me. It's got to be better in the U.S. My brother and sister lives there. Ronnie lives in New Orleans. Tio Papi Gordo sponsored Ronnie and Rakyti, but my mama has six children. I guess he could only afford two. I always wanted to believe they would come back for me. They never did.

      My girlfriend, or baby's mama as they say here, turned on me. She wants to be in the mainstream but that just doesn't matter to me. I'm a simple man. If in life I could work with my hands, have an occasional beer, and listen to Morgan Heritage blast through the speakers of my sound system, I would have lived a fulfilled life.

But of course, I wanted Marla to chase her dream. In fact, I encouraged her. She had my heart. Marla was a nursing student in Honduras. She wanted to be with a doctor or some other high positioned employee in the hospital. I'm not the professional type. I'm a laborer man– it's what I do. "Yo me voy a ir y mis hijos tambien." This is not the first time she left, but it is the last because I'm leaving too.

Lovers…half remembered
Ghosts stalks sweet love's laugh
Wintry rain sweeps darkened twilight clouds
As teardrops slowly twist the past
Lovers…half forgotten

Ronnie drove to San Antonio, Texas to pick me up. On the way, I told him how I'd hopped onto the cargo trains and witnessed others who were headed inbound US be butchered as they fell onto the tracks throughout Guatemala. I told him how we, Quinten, my younger brother who had followed me this time, and I were flagged in by the residents of Mexico, fed and offered shelter overnight for a fee. But because we didn't have money to pay or time to spend working off our debts, we jumped from the second floor window when everybody went to sleep.

I explained to him how we slept in mud piles and drunk from grimy ponds that wild animals bathe and relieved themselves in. He told me he loved me. It was good to see me.

Ronnie introduced me to his wife back at the apartment in New Orleans. She was beautiful. Kimberly was tall with a slender build, mocha tinged complexion and a size 36D. She was exactly what Ronnie talked about when we used to have heart to heart teenage boy conversations. She was his fantasy because he said not only was she gorgeous, but she is very intelligent.

"Greetings, Valentin, welcome" I just smiled and stuck my hand out to meet hers. The English language is not the easiest concept of communication for me. I understood her greetings but "Lawd, don't let her say no mo." "¿Como estas, cuñado?" "¿Tienes hambre?" she asked. "¿Que?" I said. ¡Habla espanol!" "What," I said again. "Si, Kimberly, tengo hambre pero puede ir al bano, primero." She directed me to the bathroom and headed for the kitchen to prepare a snack. This may not be so bad, I thought as I took a much needed water break. After washing up to eat I suddenly started to think, "I need a job." I guess I'm mad crazy, but I can't be without a job for more than a week. I need to do something.

On Saturday, one day after our arrival, Quinten went to New York by my sister. I met up with a couple of friends from back home that night. I was surprised to find so many Garifunas in New Orleans. I have also discovered the African history and culture held in this city. It made me aspire to learn more about my own history. I learned the Garifuna culture derived from Africans and Indians, Carib Native Americans, whose land was what we now call Honduras. Because of two sunken Spanish slave ships, Africans and Caribs co-habitated. They're language, food, and facial features among other aspects, were intertwined. "Buiti Gunoun," I spoke with Daniel in our native language. Before telling him good night, I quickly explained that I needed a job. Daniel called a few contractors who paid cash money and …I go to work on Monday.

There are six people in the two bedroom apartment I decided to share with Daniel. But it's cool, we party. Paul is a DJ, so the music blasts and the beer roll in continuously. I am having the time of my life. The United States couldn't be better" so I thought. I got tired of that life, though. I wanted a family. I miss my sons! I need to make a better life for my boys. My wife is waiting for me, but I cannot find the path to lead me to her. It sure wasn't Marla – I've been down that road. The right one is in my presence, but only if I could close my eyes and when they open I'll be standing on that road with my queen at the end. I'll find her.

A cerebral stroll we took across the Sub-Saharan region
while I was spiritually dissected and
painstakingly placed together again as one for a purpose
As I walked forward,
each step meant I was no longer the same
I was re-created for this purpose
I am, now, made from the gooey sap of submission
and the fibers of virtue
HE has made my heart pure
and able to accept and distribute
My journey had for me, sweet soil
that nourished and cooled,
brisk mental breezes sent to sustain my mental weariness
My journey had for me,

a scene that was familiar to my subconscious
My journey spoke with me and we discussed
that of which is my desire
I was taught to be found by you but
Who are you because I am waiting
My Father says wait
I have been fooled twice and joked once
waiting for you
Each time I thought my wait was to an end
but I lived a non-truth
My heart assures me that you are there
because HE has made me for you
but then…
I get confused and often burdened
because I long for you
I am slowly trailing confidence
and wondering if what my journey spoke was true
I am outfitted to be loved by you
and still, though outfitted,
I'm waiting too
I am ready and for you, I am looking to see
But My Father says wait
Because you have not found me

    On Friday nights since I've been here, we had been going to the same reggae club in New Orleans East. Crystal hung around my friends and me so much it just seemed right when she slept in my bed. She listened to reggae and spoke Spanish. We danced. I had no complaints. She was nice, but I knew I didn't walk the path and she was not my queen. She was just there ready to go out to the club. It wasn't until I noticed her getting out of bed many nights, after we went to bed, to go out with her friends that I knew I had to move.

We talked about it and disagreed and talked again. She didn't seem to hear me. Crystal was in her mid- twenties and living her life. Although, that is not very much younger than I am, I had to move. Movement is funny that way because I met Karasi at that club one night. She took my breath away. That shit was so fake to me, to hear a man say those words. It happened to me!

      She danced on air, it seemed, and smiled bright like the sun. Her long deep black locked mane bounced on her head with every turn as it played peek-a-boo with me, hiding her dazzling dark skin which glowed like onyx jade. She smelled sweet like coconuts I cracked in Truinfo. I was intrigued by her mystic beauty. ¿Quien es esa mujer? ¿Ella es de Africa?"
      This is what I asked the guy standing to my immediate left who was watching her too. To my surprise, he told me she was American and had a senseless boyfriend, but he didn't know her well enough for an introduction. We stood even closer. I wanted to know her name and what made her happy. I needed to know her life's story. I wanted to hold her hand. I found that I was on the path and she was my queen.
      I didn't even know her. How can I meet this lady? I am struggling with commanding her language. How can I successfully communicate with her? And how do I get Crystal off of me?
      She danced alone. I stood for several minutes watching for her boyfriend to come. As I hoped he never showed up, I slowly moved even closer to her. I danced with her. Looking in her eyes, we danced all night. I forgot about anyone else there. We just danced and smiled for hours. Crystal sat at the bar and watched me fall in love with this lady. 4:00 a.m. had

quickly shown itself on the clock. Karasi said, "Good night," in a very soft whisper. I felt her breath on my ear because I bent over her stature. But I felt I could never bend over her character. I heard it was too big without a word spoken by her. "What's chou name," I asked as she walked away. "Karasi and what's yours?" We began to talk. I asked for her phone number, but she questioned our ability to communicate with on the phone. I didn't care. I needed to speak with her again. Even if spangalish is what I had to speak. I wanted to see her again

Come…

listen to my voice hum
a sweet melodic tune in your eardrum
As we soar together to a new sky that shines
a thousand lights,
twirl a thousand spheres and on air,
we will begin to dance, my friend
Follow me!
Come…take my hand
Place it along side your heart
and spark the trimmer that runs down my spine
Let me feel the beat tell your time;
let me breathe your artsy essence as we sway,
Rising to the sky and fly with the songbirds
and hand in hand,
we will begin smile, my friend
Follow me!
Come…
stroke the edge of my soul
Feel the surge as I pour my honey
become your mysterious gypsy love
As I jingle the rings on my toes,
snake my globular hips,

wrap my searing wind around you
and spill out a liquid remedy for your reality
And, right at the core, we will begin to love
Follow me!
Come

Six months later...

    "Karasi, I don't think we have to leave! We'll be okay. I'm coming over to your house and we'll talk about it." It was amazing how my English improved. There was a huge storm headed for New Orleans. Karasi said people were packing and boarding up windows. She said she and her children could not stay at her house in the Ninth Ward. "It floods around here when it's a regular rainy day." She said, "I'm leaving." I was frightened to hear these words from another woman, but even still from a woman who I was convinced was to be my wife. "Well, I'm leaving too – with you!" When I arrived in New Orleans it felt as if I had entered the twilight zone. Everyone was moving about in a fast pace with petrified looks on their faces. Scores of people walked along the sidewalks or stood at the bus stops traveling to the nearest store to get goods. Bike riders carried sacks of supplies. Tons of cars filled the parking lots of Wal-Mart. People were stocking up on water, batteries, can goods and I was thinking about Karasi.

    "Does she have all of these things?" I had left work in Shreveport before receiving my check, but I had one in my pocket from the previous week. This is serious! It makes me remember the place I stood when Hurricane Mitch hit Honduras. I held my new born son for dear life in hopes that we didn't slip down in the mud as we walked in the waste deep water. I fell down holding him. I thought for sure I had lost my baby.

Marla held my other boy as everything floated into the ocean. Man, this is serious! I know this is not happening again.

I stopped at corner stores to cash my check before getting to Karasi's house. Either they wouldn't cash it or the store was closed and boarded up. She opened the door after I put one foot on the porch. This lady often scares me when she does these things. She said she's no voodoo priestess but she knows things - that's not normal. "Baby, I have a little bit money, but I have this check that I can't cash. Everything is closed!" "I have a few dollars, it's okay," she said after she kissed me. "Do you still want to leave?" I wanted to know her plans and assist her with whatever she needed. "Yeah, but I just got Lulu from the hospital and my mama is tripping. I want to see what they're going to do before I leave."

Karasi called everybody in her phonebook, warning them about leaving the city. It was Saturday. Instead of being at City Park where she usually is on Saturdays, this lady was sitting or pacing with a phone receiver to her ear. I'd never seen her like this. The volunteer evacuation became a mandatory one by night fall. The next morning I woke up to find Karasi packing and still on the phone. "Baby we gotta go," she said.

Trey was walking behind her. That's my little man, Trey. He's a big, little dude. "Mommy, where we going?" It was 5:30 in the morning but Trey smells his mama, I think. All she would have to do is walk pass his room. He was walking behind her with a medium sized luggage bag, helping his mama.

I stayed in the bed trying to make myself believe I wanted to leave the city. Shreveport was a ride that exhausted me and I had just come from there. I jumped up with false energy because there was no changing this lady's mind. At about 8:00a.m., I heard her voice tremble as she spoke on the phone. I walked to the living room where she stood in the middle of the floor. She was talking to Ms. Amina. I can't touch that! Whenever she and her mother talk to each other I have learned to stay out of it.

I remained quiet until they finished but what I didn't know is that they would never finish that conversation. I loaded her car with our clothes and cooler that filled the car to its storage capacity not knowing what event would come next. Where am I allowing this lady to take me; I have no legal identity in this country.

Karasi drove to her mother's.

Walking through a tunnel of darkness,
deafening sounds rush to the delicate ear
Step by extremely elongated step - one trembles with fear
FLASH! then suddenly a radiant beam of light crashes unto the infirm eye, folding up with excruciating pain, your head feels as if it's moving rapidly in a gyrate motion but there are no tears to cry
With blurred vision you think your coming to an end, as quickly as your feet move it's getting further and further away
FASTER! the sound of pitter-patter moves
as swift as an arrow
but still leaving you in dismay
The unrestrained pursuit of pleasure nags at you
as you enter darkness once again
while perceiving disillusion,

*Don't be afraid,
It's only a way of life
Livin' in confusion*

Chapter Eight

Bruce "Boogie" Thibodeaux

Man, that girl is crazy! She come in here early in the morning talkin' 'bout, "Get up, please! We have to go." I turned over, me. "Bruce, what are you going to do? New Orleans has never had a category five hurricane and I know it won't be safe. I feel it."

Is she serious? It's Sunday morning. "I'm tired – I ain't goin' nowhere." She talking 'bout what she feel. I told my mama somp um wrong with her. She ain't right. "Go head, Karasi. Leave me 'lone na." She walked to the back of the house to my mama's room. I heard her waaayyy up here. "I called you and you said you would be ready." "We going to the Superdome..." my mama said. That was it for me. I closed my eyes.

I grew up knowing my sister, who is eight years older than me, had some problems. She beat people up. That worked for me because at school I told everybody my sister was crazy and they better not mess with me. As I grew older, I started to understand her more and we became friends. I mean, we were brother and sister, but she became my friend as I grew older. I knew she loved me, but she never would say it. I thought because she didn't like my daddy, she didn't like me either.

I started to resent my daddy for her, but I never really understood why she had so much animosity toward him. I remember when we lived in Eastsho'. I was still in elementary school and Karasi had just graduated high school. She was trying to be an open hearted and kind person. I knew her well. She wanted to go to Baton Rouge for SU football game. Karasi had dance school that Saturday morning, and after class she came back to start sweeping and vacuuming before my mama got home. My mama came back from making groceries later.

Karasi asked her for permission to go to the game. Well, my mama was from the old school, pretty much. Karsai's boyfriend was in the band at Southern University in Baton Rouge so my mama said "no!" "You ain't going waaayy to Baton Rouge to get pregnant!" All hell broke loose! Karasi went to screaming.

"What do you think of me? I want to see the game; really I want to listen to the band because no one really watches the game. I want to go with my friends and yes, Edward will be there, but he will be with his friends too. We don't get down like that anyway."

My mama said, no again. Karasi went off! "I graduated from school, ya heard me, and if you don't trust me that's your problem – I'm going to the game."

She started packing. My sister moved to Baton Rouge that fall. Edward and Shelley were enrolled at SU that semester and they both had their own apartment. She called Edward to pick her up. He came all the way from Baton Rouge to get her. They were more brother and sister than boyfriend and girlfriend. Shelley shoulda been my sister too! Her and my sister was tight. You know they say when you mess up, an associate will be there to tell you about it but if the same situation jumped off, a true friend will be in that mess with you and be there to tell you how y'all made a mess of that one.

Shelley was cool, man. She always had a smile on her face – Karasi too – which made me know they both were crazy. They could be pissed off and smiling. Boy look, I got outta their way. They wasn't like that much though. They laughed a lot, goofy that's what they were. I had two sisters, Karasi and Shelley. They were gone.

My sister called home for me from time to time. I missed her so much that I ain't want to do nothin'. My mama told her that I wasn't doing well in school, if I even went, and it was her fault. My sister really didn't care that she said it was her fault, but she always talked to me about school. She came home. She hugged me and said, "I love you and I will never leave you alone here." I knew she was directing that toward my daddy. But I didn't exactly know what she meant. Anyway, I was glad that she was home.

We went back to our old selves, fussing and fighting but loving one another. When time came, my sister explained to me that she had to go away to college. She was going to Jackson State. She promised that she would call, and I grew up without her in the same household, at that point, because even when she wasn't in school, she wasn't at the house with my mama and daddy.

She lived with Shelley and her family pretty much since she was in junior high school. I felt her love anyway. I remembered the things she would say to me. I got into that Talib Kweli and Common; she told me 'bout these cats. I witnessed those situations she warned me about. I knew how to handle them and move on.

Hmm he wondered

Wondered what you saw when you looked at his shoes
They're not worn but brand new
Did you think he was the same guy you saw on the news?
Or did you choose to case his outer surface?
Hmmm he wondered

*Wondered what you felt when you backed up a pace
when he came near
Did you fear him? Or did you clear the path
so he could walk by?
Hmmm he wondered
but knew you judged his color
which no other man there shared
Slacks and coat, shirt and tie –
white face, red hair, blue eyes
Spewing out no discrimination lies
You judged his persona from your brain dead stereo-
type
that earned your KKK stripes
Your granddaddy's daddy wish is what you live by
but slavery days are no longer
Hmmm he wondered
and met your stare with a deportment
that was burly yet mellow
So you stuck your hand out, greeted him with a smile
and said "hello"*
CORPORATE AMERICA

Karasi came back to the front with bags in her hand. With her foot on my throat, she told me she needed me to open my trunk because our stuff won't fit in her car. "Wait a minute, I ain't going nowhere! Give me my damn keys!" This is what I yelled as I stomped to the back to see what my mama was talking about.

"We're going to just ride out far enough to be away from the storm and come back," she said. So I stomped back to the front room to grab my play station and Kenneth Coles – and woke Love up. Man, the wrath from waking that woman up!

After we hopped in the cars, we stopped over at my mother- in- law's house to see about the dog. Ya know we left him some water and food, played with him for a while. By that time, Karasi was blowing her horn ridiculously while bumping that Mos Def. I came out jukking, dancing to "I am the most beautiful Boogie Man, the most beautiful Boogie Man. Let me be your favorite nightmare. Close your eyes and I'll be right there."

We were on the road. I was sleepy. Brotha had a hard night!

Chapter Nine

Tia Burgundi Bostich

Adhere to the lessons echoed from the graceful walls,
listen to the water muttered sacrificial calls,
feel the wind rush through to the bone,
humble your tone
as you enter the mystic silk cave
It is there, where, the first offering is held,
it is there, where,
the truth is archived,
it is there,
where, the future us…saved
She took me there - and we twirled around the sun,
the moon and the earth;
It was there,
where, I witnessed the sea's breeze,
the flame of obliteration,
the drops of liquid requisite that worked as one for life
It was there where,
I smelled the spiritual bouquet held by Osun,
It was there where
I helped churn this black and red and green clay-like
stuff with Imhotep that later became a nation sharp
as a knife
To cut through time, to slice the unwanted away,
to puncture all of the fearless kind,
to engrave a life sized print at the bay
It was there,
in the cave, where, I started to become confused
for inside of this diminutive casing were
tall trees and wide seas,
boisterous fires and plentiful leaves

which were replicating tall trees and wide seas,
boisterous fires
and plentiful leaves
It was there, in the cave, where,
I started to become confused
because they sang loudly and drummed hysterically,
and looped each other in a million frenzies or mo'
It was there, in the cave, where, I began to glow
And frightened, I ran to her
And she stroked my little hand,
and brushed back my mahogany,
thick, coarse hair
Then she lifted me in her arms
and extended them to the heavens
and I grew and became ample and... cried
because it was there, that, I realized
I was this nation's first offering...
a small slave girl turned powerful woman...
I surrender
I surrender to the first offering

    My name is Tia Burgundi Sevory? Bostich?. My biological father's last name is Sevory. I have never seen him before in my life. I was told he lives in Arizona. My Grammy told me he is from Mississippi. My mama, well, she answers my questions very matter of factly, oftentimes with one or two words. Sometimes I write those words down because I think if I put them together I will get a whole story that explains to me the reason sadness swaddles her face when I ask anything about my father. She said he cheated on her while she carried me. I put that together after three conversations. He cheated with his girlfriend before my mother. Eventually my mother learned of this deceit.

    My mother started to dress up for him and make sure the house was orderly. But he would pick fights with her accusing her of dressing pretty for someone else while he was away at work. He told her that she was fat and he wasn't buying any maternity clothes for her like it was some sort of punishment for talking back to him.

She became very depressed after putting him out of her studio apartment. My mother said she cried and cried. My Grammy said she acted as if she was dead. My Uncle Boogie said he overheard her tell my Nanny Shelley she wished she was dead. Nanny Shelley came to our house everyday to make mama laugh. It was strange that it never worked at that time. My Nanny Shelley was funny! They were good friends – like sisters. My mother was hurting and my Nanny was too. When I was born I had two mothers. Although my mama called to Mr. Sevory in Arizona from the hospital, I never had a father. I had Mama and Nanny Shelley.

My mama started coming around little by little but never, my uncle said, never like before. He knew something was still wrong. Just as I started to walk at nine months, my mother attempted to take her own life. She said life just wasn't for her and she was tired. Grammy said she was always a depressed child. She wore black and covered her bedroom windows to hide the day light after her daddy died.

They said she was so emotional, moody emotional, as a teenager. As she sat on the floor, in dark, with a razor in her hand and many others on the floor, I touched her, she said. She thought I was in my baby bed. She said I walked through the house, in dark, and found her behind the dining room table at three o'clock a.m. and touched her. "You were sent to save my life. You were given to me, a gift to love, maybe you were sent by my daddy." This is what she told me as she wept one day. I know she was trying to tell me this story but I got it already, in fragments.

Confusion tells me

that I don't want to be in holy matrimony
because loneliness haunts my soul
and unfaithfulness is in my spirit
Neglect shows me that I am not your first priority
neither am I your first pick of family
for your family consist of people far away
I cannot be them nor they me
Suffocated love tells me that I am dying
I am no longer the same blossoming woman
I am walking dead
I cannot breathe – I am not nourished – I cannot be!
I have made the biggest mistake yet - times two
For the next mistake came
when the baby I am carrying was conceived with you
What a blessing to have possessed
the ability to bring forth life?
What pain to have acquired a numbed heart?
What am I to do about the curse
of the unhappy pot bellied wife?
What detriment to have a home falling apart?

As I take a step and render forth my hand
As I cover my mouth with hopes of savored breath
I am not able to stand the backwoods and wastelands
of the field that I am standing alone
Alone with a fertilized egg in my womb
and a susceptible baby at my side
Fighting the strong gusts of thick winds
while scooping her up in my wing
I am dying!
Rubbing my stomach filled with mixed emotions

Laced Bloodline

realizing the thomp I just felt was my unborn –
sworn to nurture by nature
I love this child
I don't see you
but I hear the empty promises
of which comes from your gut
Wearied I take another step,
survival envelops my energy given
never ceasing to try
but my daughter is watching me die
Loneliness hovers over my soul
and faithfulness is far gone from my heart
Just as maturity has gone from you
as responsibility dangles at your outskirts
bouncing off as your sights are filled with glitter
Can't you speak without lying
about the un-necessities you are buying
Can't you see your every word cracks the essence of
me
I am dying.
I am dying.
I am dying.
You are killing me with kindness
because reality you just don't know
I am not in your fantasy
I live amongst the world flow
And I cannot live alone
As the man, my husband and this is your home –
this is where responsibility lives and I cannot live alone
Here is where I stop, on the side of the road, choking,
with my child and my unborn, crying
In this smog filled existence, we are dying!
And we are alone

    Bostich was the name of my brother's father. He was my mother's husband once. But I watched her die inside over and over. I was so afraid she could be back to the place where she was once. She made a promise to me though. Because I was given to her to love, she said, a spiritual gift to remind her of the importance of life, she promised to never go back there. My mother, if giving her word, sticks to her word. She gave me her word.

She carried me under her broken wings and stepped out on faith and her word. I still feel like she doesn't love me sometimes. She assures me that I am her baby, her first baby. She says sometimes her heart gets so overwhelmed that it makes her explode inwardly. I guess these are the times when she yells at me or pushes me away. She doesn't do dainty girl stuff but she tries. I guess I'll understand one day. But she says she's not a girl's mom, but she loves me. I love her too.

I never really say too much because my mama tells me to be quiet a lot. But on the morning we packed up and went by Grammy, I didn't know what to say. My mama asked me again and again what was wrong. I had nothing to say – she said that was a first.

I didn't know whether to be afraid or calm knowing she would take care of me. I knew Lulu was going to die because she had the same thing that killed my Nanny Shelley. I knew that Uncle Boogie wasn't going anywhere; it was too early. I, however, didn't know what my mama was going to do.

She said everybody have to go! She said it with her "I'm not playing, do what I say" look. I guess I was just quiet because I knew better than to say anything that may be the wrong thing to say. I was quiet until I had to go to a new school in Texas. I made new friends and rode a school bus. At home in New Orleans, there weren't any school busses to bring me to school and take me home after school was over. My new friends spoke Spanish. I was happy.

It was almost like my old school where we learned everything in Spanish. They gave me uniforms and shoes. My mama said we didn't have those things anymore. My friends gave me everything I needed for school. They were nice. On Thursdays, at school, a production from a local church would visit. They preformed spiritual skits about everyday life and obstacles. The non-denominational skits taught us how to overcome hardships from peer pressure, sharing, compromise – most of the things my mama talks about at home. I liked my new school.

We even started going to the church. My family smiled again. That was until my mama received a phone call from the missing persons people. They asked her if she knew Tia Burgundi. It turned out that Mr. Sevory had reported me missing. I had never seen this man before in my life. He never called me on any of my eight birthdays. "What the hell does he want?!!!" That's what my mama asked the lady from Missing Persons. "Tell him my daughter is alright and she has been alright for the past eight years…and by the way, tell him she'll be nine years old next month and has never even heard his voice! What does he want? Money, shit?! Does he want FEMA money, for a daughter he has never seen, except on a picture? Certainly he is not concerned, so what the hell does he want?!" The voice on the receiving end was astounded, I'd imagine.

She paused and after my mama shouted "hello," she asked if she could report our whereabouts to him. Again, my mama shouted "No!" That was the end of that.

I can't wait to go back to Texas. I'ma ask my mama if I can go to my school and see my friends, especially Carla. Huh!? We have to live in a hotel again in New Orleans. I don't know why we have to stay here. It is dirty and nothing is open. We can't go to the park to play because people are there living in trailers. We can't go to African dance class anymore because everybody is somewhere else. I hate this stupid school my mama is making me go to – the people are nice, except my teacher. I miss my school in Texas. So I still don't say anything just like the morning we left this place.

Chapter Ten

Amina Thibodeaux

"I'm not going nowhere." I remember Hurricane Betsy. My daddy went around getting people with his boat because water was at the roof tops. The levee had broken in the Ninth Ward, nothing can be worse than that. This will be just like the rest of the times when everyone got scared for nothing. My daughter seems to be losing her mind. She thinks dooms day is coming. Every time the phone rings, Karasi is on the other end. "Get the hell off my phone, girl. Stop calling me!" It's so easy to hurt her feelings, but she is persistent whether her feelings are hurt or not. "What are we going to do with Lulu, Karasi?" Before I knew it, my baby was at my door coming to carry us away. "By any means necessary" she said.

I'm shol glad she put up such a fuss. New Orleans was a mess when those levees broke. People's bodies were floating or being eaten by alligators, I heard. Lawd, have mercy, my child got us out of there. I asked her before leaving, what are we going to do with Lulu but if we were still there, Jesus...

Karasi grew up as a troubled child. I thought it was due to the brain tumor. Most of her life, she has been telling me that I was wrong. She assured me that she is stronger than a label. She refused to be labeled by anyone, even me. I never really understood my child but I love her wholeheartedly.

I thought she had no love for me at one point in her life. This storm has erased all doubt in mind. Now I know Karasi would give her life for me and her babies. She carries the weight of the family on her shoulders.

It's almost like she has the spirit of my daddy inside of her.

Once upon a storybook love,

when daffodils swayed and humming birds sang,
a girl's warm heart was filled
with the harmony of a symphony
When the stars glistened like diamonds
and air smelled of natural perfume, she smiled
Once upon a storybook love

Once upon a twisted fairytale,
when shrieks of hatred soared through the streets
and trees bared "strange fruit"
that woman mourned truth
When bullets reign the air
and fire brightened the night, she cried
Once upon a twisted fairytale
Based on a true story

Never in a million years would I have moved to Texas. I have found good in the midst of this terrible phenomenon. My husband is here and seems to be a better person. Lawd knows we've had our battles. He takes care of me. These days I have been so weary and forgetful. I don't know whether I'm coming or going.

     My daddy is gone. My sister is gone. My mama is gone. I feel alone at times. I never talked to Karasi about what was troubling me. She is my daughter not my friend, I thought. But I know a little better. My Karasi is grown now with babies of her own.

     She talks to me about subjects she has never shared allowing me to engage in a healthy conversation with her, woman to woman. I told her that I am scared. After the stroke, I am just not the same. I have no outward disabilities, all of my extremities are functioning, but my memory and focus are diminishing.

When I listen to her tell me about my experience in the hospital (I don't remember any of it), it frightens me even more. Karasi's belief is, although I went through that dark passage way, it wasn't my time. She said I had unfinished business and God sent back me for that reason. Since then, I was given a chance to dance at my daughter's 31st birthday party. I was given the opportunity to bid my daddy farewell after I had done all that was in my power to make him comfortable while he was in hospice. I have nursed my mother until her final sleep. I have gotten my thoughtful husband back, the man I married twenty something years ago. And he is getting on my damn nerves, but I like it.

I have visited a farm with animals I would have never been close to in my life. I am living and laughing – this is what Karasi meant. Katrina gave me the opportunity to smell the flowers and breathe.

Yesterday I cried
Because my feet were dried and cracked
Because my eyes were weary and blackened
Because in my heart was a splintering pain for my children
Because the fruit I bared for you withered and died
I loved you as a mother of nature
and never before but…
Yesterday I cried
Because you stopped loving me

In My Journal

"Dreaming Me"

"Up you mighty race, accomplish what you will" Marcus Garvey

There are times when our confidence fail and every unnecessary obstacle block our path. This is when we must move from the place that burdens us. We must create a vehicle to remove us from what hinders aspiration or physical gifts that we have worked so hard to receive. Some of us will work all of our lives for some physical attribute and just as hard work pays off, it's lost. This doesn't mean that dreams are lost. It doesn't mean life is lost. It only means that we must move and keep moving forward.

Never are we to give up!
Never are we to allow ourselves to be defeated!
We are beautiful beings created by God.
We are victorious!
We are strong!
We are precious in everything!
We are royalty!
God's people

"Embraced Dream"

I dream of rivers

Ancient, muddy, stretched rivers
The Nile flowing near the temple of Isis
The Congo passing through Kinshasa
I dream of rivers
I dream of wading in the water
by the riverside in the ancient rivers

I dream of Solomon and Makeda
The bond formed between Ethiopians
and Israelites
I dream of the black beauty as Solomon
lusted for her
The son created by them
and great nations thereafter
I dream of Solomon and Makeda
I dream of sitting at the feet of Menelik

I lay my head upon a wooden pillow
and inhale the struggle of a Nubian Nation
as dirt pebbles burden my flesh
I dream of the Sahara when it wasn't a desert

Send me the pillow that you dream on
So that I can dream on it too
I heard a man say
But can my dreams fit on your pillow?

I dream of Oshun
Of her lessons of vanity
Of her yellow and gold wardrobe
I dream of Xango

I dream of Kemit
And the black soil of today's Egypt
I dream of Nubia
The black man land

*I physically slumber
and mentally live
in olden times of the African world*

*I sleep on the concrete faced up,
arms stretched wide
As my slobber drips into the mold
and then seeps onto the earth
And I hear the chants of the ancestors*

*Send me the pillow that you dream on
But can your pillow fit my dreams?*

"Nobody loves a little black girl when she becomes a woman"

Pampered and loved, guided and cherished, is the treatment of the little ebon princess, being taught right from wrong, heavenly from evil and catered to in the process

As she grows older and knowledge begins to expand and in society's eyes she's all grown up, no one can see the person within, yet there are still blessings filling her cup because no one knows what she feels inside, the only means of sanity she knows is to hide, to shy away from the world, to protect that helpless little girl that was loved and now all alone, from society withdrawn

She, who now feels into a corner she's backed so just like a panther she's ready to attack - anyone who comes near, she'll fear knowing they would somehow hurt her and bid her strife so to get near her you'll have to give her your life

No one loves a black little girl when she becomes a woman – like two negative forces that rebels against all men because they tend to abuse their own and worship other cultures and crush their pride and confidence she has within so she's never caring but approaching her you may but if she strikes at you with anger, remember you made her that way!   Society

"The Fault is Mine"

*For trusting, for talking, for giving them my time
The fault is mine
For dividing my passions to accommodate then combining distortion as
one
For changing the moon to the sun, convincing myself of thinking
everything is fine
The fault is mine*

"DEEP, DARK, CHOCOLATE CUP O' TEA"

*Steam fills the small romantic café
as jazz music caress my ear lobe along with a
romp pa domp
strong beat of his tender palms
meeting the drum
Mist on the top of my lip as I sipped
my tea and listened
watched him glide to the oval table
topped with a jarred candle
as I sat there with a quivering gut
because here comes my SECRET
secret because no one knows…….not even him*

Laced Bloodline

*He took a seat so near
he tasted my feminine soul
he felt my gentle invitation to intertwine
MY MIND WANDERED
as I wished I had a cup o' tea -
deep, dark, chocolate cup o' tea
"T" is sweet isn't he?
the one who shares his intimacy
some where's else
Isn't he taken by the attraction of another sister
isn't he………………………Gorgeous
distance is my defense against
my overwhelmed passion,
against his smile
distance saves me…
I have much respect for my…sisters*

*There was a ring on my napkin
from the sweaty mug,
just as clammy as my skin is,
as I attempted to converse with this brother
and not gaze at him (I think I did anyway)
As I studied his outward perfection
and weighed them
with his outward imperfection…
as I learned his soul…perfect!
Dark - and - Locked –
and - Deep Eyes   Gorgeous
"Can I get you something?"
 it was the waitress talking
as he glided back over to his drum
"Sister, can I get you anything?"
she said, as she turned to see where my gaze led
" A deep, dark, chocolate cup o' tea"
I said a little above a whisper
"We have herbal, raspberry,*

green but no chocolate"
very apologetic, she said
I replied, "It's okay I can't have him anyway"
I, then, walked to the door with my keys…
and left

"Unwillingly Devoted"

Sometimes my conscious says stay away from the touch that draws you near,

the words you love to hear, the smile you adore so dearly…just attracts me

Sometimes my heart cries, "You'll be hurt by lies, Don't be fooled by a love as high as the sky," a feeling so lovely…just attracts me

Sometimes my soul yearns for a desire that burns, his every sensitive spot wanting to learn, stimuli forced so strongly…just attracts me

Even though I try, scream and cry not to fall so quickly

Still…just attracts me

Sometimes skeptical thoughts roam the dark paths and smother the touched base reality and sometimes, though unwillingly, you attract me

"He Makes Love to Me"

He makes love to me
with no physical touch
but in such a way my core covets

Laced Bloodline

He takes me soaring high
I shudder as his voice launches
vibrations to my spine
I arch my back to his every oral caress
I rest my thighs
and wrap my arms around his cleverness
I open my heart
I open my essence
Open to his visions as he receives mine
Open to his dreams
as we entwine our minds, our spirits,
Our souls embrace
He makes love to me

I'm diggin' you
like deep tombs hidden, holding pharaohs
Like the cacti spines in the sands
blowing over the Serengeti
I know you
like the orange flames
that flicker through candle wax
like the patterns on my palm
like electric currents when the switch is on
I taste you
Like coconut milk soaked Techini
Like cooked praline sugar
Like vinegar covered beets

I take a deep breath
and exhale the sheer essence of your spirit
I take a deep breath and sigh

You in me
Like the words that lived in Harlem
during the renaissance
Like the black skin I wear

Like
  …damn
dried mucus balls in the nose
Like cheese in the toes
Like my tooth wearing taffy candy
Like loose satin panties
I'm diggin' you
…out!

"SELF-ESTEEM ISSUE"

HE SAID, (WITH A CURIOUS TONE) "HELLO" TO A LONELY HEART

HE CARESSED A BLISTERING SORE NEVER SEEN EVEN WITH THE KEENEST SIGHT - THE FIGHT INSIDE BEGAN IT'S VOICE OF RESONANCE AS PROCEEDING WITH A CLOSER STEP TO HIS APPROACH WITH SKEPTICISM AS HE REACHED TO FONDLE THE DARK HE SAID, (WITH A CURIOUS TONE) "HELLO"

HE GAVE A NUMBER AND SAID,"WHEN YOU FEEL LIKE SOME OF ME, COME AND GET ME"

HE SAID,"HAVE YOU EVER THOUGHT ABOUT YOUR THIGH ON MINE" OR "MY BREATHE ON YOUR EAR"

FEAR OF CLOSENESS STRUCK BUT QUICKLY ENDED IN DEFEAT BY COMFORT

HE SAID, "I LIKE YOUR LASHES" - UNDER THE GLASSES PASSES THROUGH THE BANKS - A

FESTERING HOLE IN THE SOUL HE SAW - FELT AS HE MASSAGED AWAY THE PRESSURES OF LIFE

FOR THAT MOMENT RELEASING THE BLARING YELPS ALWAYS HEARD

FOR THAT MOMENT RELEASING THE VICIOUS ATTACKS SENT BY ONLY ONE WORD

HE SAID, "I LIKE YOUR BOSOM" AS HE HELD A WOUNDED SPIRIT IN A TIME OF TURMOIL HE AIRED A SOILED WOMB WITH HESITATED APPROVAL STUMBLING TOWARD WHAT FELT SO DAMN GOOD AND BRUSHING THE BARENESS AGAINST HIS BEARD HE SAID, "HOW LONG HAS IT BEEN?"

OUT OF A PUNCTURED HEART HE PULLED A HOOK AND WITH MY CURIOUS LOOK

HE SAID,
"GOODNIGHT"

"Perhaps with you"

Complete happiness I would know perhaps…
Sometimes I drift to avoid dismay
I become numb to emotion,
for I have come
to accept people for people
but with you perhaps…
I would smile in the depths
for that I have never known
…but perhaps with you

Imagine

The Making Of…

Thuds of colored drops of rain
plummeting takes me to the place
where my ancestors lay.
They comfort me as they chant
harmonious knowledge
They play me like the woman, Djembe
They tell me of my kind
who shared my dreams long ago,
who pre-molded my mind just as warm clay.
They sing…
They pacify my wounds
when happiness culminates

The cool from the sweltering sun renews my soul
 when the dried asphalt at my feet tickle
Tickles, as my toes wiggle a dance of freedom
Shining from the imperceptible gold
my father bestow upon me,
I sing…
My kin of yester reserves my soul
They settle in to the core
We sing…
 I am them

"Calling the Harvest to Refuge"

Territorial Green Vultures…imagine
Straining the energy which adorns
the heart beat
tiny fraction of life-chiseled,
rotted like meat, sweet as kraut
clout hunters-X marks the spot

Laced Bloodline

*but not the punter of the ball
fall to the knees constant-ly
be walked on the side,
stride with no hip, smothered like a chop of pork,
no yolk, just coke-cane to nourish the fetus
feed us no knowledge but trashy news - media
needing a barrel with wheel
to haul the steel plated from the bull
full of contempt, anxiety
soulless wimp pimp the beauty
that misplace her royalty
loyalty to the poisoned filled cigar-rette,
pipe, syringe,
cringe at the thought of being pure
pour the boric acid on the brain
that sends shocks to the temple!
simple-minded, with scholar potential,
with maggot stenciled on the heart
apart from the sense of feel
"Peel the mask"
My dream said in the night
or the night said to my daydream,
Or was it a dream?
So confused,
abused by my own people
as they abuse themselves
Sells liquid bullets
sells powered attacks to the heart - smart
But can't see, we can't see high
Drugged out on the program
or hiding from the real
Scared, ready to jump out and into skin paled*

*American embryo, been that way raised
Dislocated student, heard that way speak...
but just peak into the womb of Mother Africa*

Climb
Launch unto the umbilical cord wet
Accept her amniotic knowledge,
she's calling her seeds- hear her
She's taking back her lost
but erect muscles spit at her
as he enters orgasmic disrespect
But pulsating climaxes squeezes her tongue
But the needle punctures her veins
and fills them with toxin
But the artificial, lubricating,
chemical grease destroys her hair
But the plastic pupils blinds her eyes
But the acrylic disfigures her fingers
As there on the horizon sits Mother Africa
She waits, she cries,
she feels the slaps to her cheeks
She knows some may never unveil
But yet, she waits and whispers in the night,
in my dream,
to my people
"Peel the mask"

"Introducing Me"

Truth is…
I am but what you see
There's not a special fiber that made me
I am but what I say
There's not a wicked utterance from my gut
I have but one face
and my mouth is placed
not differently than yours
But difference shows my mouth stores
the words you hate to hear

You fear the truth,
the very entity my soul feeds to
True to my core, true to my ethos
hunger for the knowledge of our intimates
I am the slime you stepped in when
the historia itch filled your being
I am the haze in your dream
when you grasped onto your Africana roots,
The vine you climb fleeing assimilation,
the very strings holding up your boots
I am the voice inside that whispers
speak your mind, feel your heart,
taste your vibes,
smell the aroma of truth because I am tired
Of brothas disrespecting sistahs
that would make the next sistah weary
to be one of you
so she chooses blue eyes, straight hair,
bleach her skin so fair but I am
In love with my people
I am like Dorothy and Toto
circling in the tornado and off to see
the wizard when I think of this blizzard
we call life
I am Nena, Nena, speak Nena
I am great-granddaughters
of the daughters of Nubia
I am the one who vowed to be true to ya
Creator's divine creation, most sacred property
Truth is…that be

"May I Have A Word"

As long as the world exists

To the prejudice white man,

Don't be upset with me because you can't be as fortunate as we who are of color, because you are not my brother. Don't be upset with me because you can't be as fortunate as we who stick together with our creed, because we all breathe the same air and accept each other as one and from your world of segregation we did not run. Don't be afraid of me because I am different and understanding you can't see. Don't be afraid or upset because God took time to color me.

From the depths,
A mighty race

Chapter Eleven

The Gumbo Bowl

It is April, the most beautiful spring month I've witnessed in New Orleans. The weather is breezy and sunny. It is just beautiful! I had begun planning an event that would soon change my life. I am planning a wedding. But preparing for a wedding does not bother me nearly as much as the hesitation to redevelop my beloved city in its entirety.

Lulu's heart would have been broken had she seen this mess. I am unable to sleep with worry of the possibility of a failed attempt to rebuild my home. I am unable to sleep with worry concerning the trickery I have to battle to save my grandparent's land. The, seemingly, true definition of the American way is bare in the southern region of the country. The discrimination that lived dormant was washed up and exposed as Katrina saturated southern soil.

Louisiana's state government seems to be pulling blind folds over the eyes of the city government. The Federal Government seems to be evading their responsibilities which are the levees. They are playing tug of war with the governor of Louisiana. So, because of this rat race and my search for stability, I continued to place the life I lived in my head on the pages of my journal.

As Kolunde held Tiye, to send with her well wishes for the night, she allowed her body to be seen with a touch when he closed his eyes. She shared her soft caresses that were saved for him but rationed for their lengthy goodnight or morning hugs. At those times they held the most intimate conversations. He told her how much he yearned for a woman who was an extension of him but a nurturer, care giver.

With his eyes closed, he told her she was beautiful when he leaned toward her, carefully, making sure to never physically touch her. But leaning close enough for them to smell the fragrance of lust in the air they were breathing. Tiye was paralyzed at these times. She longed for him to remove the elusive fence that held her on the friendship block of their build-a-relationship game board. But he just kept her there, at friendship, gazing at her and hugging her.

Kolunde was a concert promoter. He traveled often to view potential venues for shows. Although, he booked the biggest names in hip hop, he scouted venues that were in areas known to be violent and impoverished. This is where hip hop progressed and this is where hip hop is appreciated the most because it is where the lyrics are born. This is where people knew what it was to be hungry, to survive the struggle.

He dealt with many artists but they had to be special kind of artists who had not been changed into a "larger than the Creator" life form. They had to be people who live their lyrics and send positive messages through their songs. In Tiye's eyes, Kolunde was a decent brotha. He was sensitive but strong, mellow but mighty, and passionate about his people.

~~~~~~~~~~~~~~~~~~~~~~~~~~~

She went to the concerts that were no more than three hours away. True, it was because she loved the music, but also because she felt Kolunde's presence in her soul whenever she was next to anything he touched.

We shared stories from back in the day when hip hop was our life. We shared stories expressing what truly was the making of the person standing before me or the making of the person standing before him. We shared recipes, instruments, ideas, and concerns. I shared my heart. And he knew!

I believe he knew of all the guarded love I detained. It was amazing how I expected this man to know what was inside of me. After all, he was just learning me. I was learning him but absorbed more of his soul with each communicable moment. There was a sad place in his soul that I wanted to exuberate. I wanted him to know my wounds. I wanted him to know my insecurities. I wanted him to know my heart; the cut out had been measured and tailored for him. He is in my dreams.

~~~~~~~~~~~~~~~~~~~~~~~~~~

"As we swayed, standing on clouds and listening to the African sounds of Alpha Blondy delicately roving through the atmosphere, we smiled. We walked, together, on the edges of paradise, hand in hand, without a word uttered but a soothing vibe that told a million stories. With your eyes, you told me that I am your wife, as you rubbed your hand along the nap of my neck.
And I, quivering inside as I slightly rolled my neck leaning toward what felt so damn good. My hair became exposed and it began to cover my face. But you brushed it away and stared. Still without a word, you moved your hand though my natural tresses with one hand and gently grasped my waist with the other.

I slowly moved to the chimes of the melody playing. There we stood on the edge of paradise, wanting, in my dream."

~~~~~~~~~~~~~~~~~~~~~~~~~~

On the corner of St. Claude Ave. and Alabo in the CTC (cross the canal, New Orleans' lower ninth ward), my cousin and I would stand choosing cars as they zoomed by to have as our own. I always chose the older modeled cars. My mama say, I was an old soul since birth. The ancestors have walked with me ever since. We played marbles in the dirt next to the tracks, but as little dudes we often had real big men ideas.

I told my cousin I was going to spread positive energy throughout the world through some kind of art form; I just wasn't sure which art form. I told him that I smell death and our people are killing themselves. We listened to Triggerman on a cassette tape playing in our boom box. As we bobbed our heads and plucked marbles, we made a pact to always spread the good word.

I watched my sister submit to the ways of a two cent prostitute so she could get high. She started robbing people, killing people, and blowing her punk ass two bit pimp when he was tired of her vagina that had only been innocent for the first year of her life. She came home pregnant! My mama hadn't seen her for four months. But "she popped up pregnant," my mama said.

I had seen her. I used to follow her when she went on her escapades. Tamalah never knew though. I was eleven years old; she was sixteen and I wanted to know why she wasn't at home. I watched her make her money. I watched her buy her heroin or crack somebody in the head for their wallet but, then get strong armed and raped.

I went to take up for her all of the time. She would be so high she never even knew I was there. I wanted to protect her, but her friends would just push me to the ground and call my sister all kind of jacked up names. They told me that I would be just like her. An addict. I ran whenever I saw a gun, ran all the way home to my daddy to tell him what I had seen Tamalah do.

He told me, very calmly and matter of factly, "Your sister is dead." But Daddy...all it took was for him to raise his hand and I was silenced. I remember when he told me he would kill me if I told him anything else about my sister. I believed him. My sister has hurt him so much that in his mind he rather know her as dead than a living mistake of his, tarnished with the family's secret.

He blamed himself for my sister's addiction. "Why my baby!" I heard him cry out to seemingly no one one night as I peeked through the curtain that separated the hall from the living room where I slept. He was on his knees and then his stomach, stretched out flat, wailing and vomiting because he was drunk. "I trusted that bastard to babysit," my daddy blurted out often, but I never knew what he was talking about.

Due to a computer error that let him out early, my father had just come home from Angola for shooting his brother to death for raping his daughter. Tamalah was two and my cousin, Sage, was born that year. He was born three years before me, but he carried such wisdom that made him seem a whole lot older. When his daddy died, his mama killed herself so my mama took him as her own. Sage would tell me about him and Tamalah growing up. He said he hated her because she was the reason his father was gone. And that he hated my daddy because he killed his daddy. I would just shake my head and fold my arms because I knew this dude wasn't gon' sit there on those tracks and tell me that he hated my mama too! If it wasn't for her he would surely be missing.

But he would say he loved my mama and that it was confusing to him. How could she love him after what happened? He said, my mother told him, "This is what's going to happen, African child. You will be a respectful and well respected man. You will have a heart filled with love and I will love you forever, my son."

He said, Tamalah was a jewel to my mama, but she was eccentric to him. She was nervous all of the time. She shook with tremors involuntarily. "Po' thang!"

Sage told me what he overheard the grownups in the neighborhood talking about. My mama found Tamalah, one day, in the closet in my uncle's room bleeding from her mouth and her private parts. Uncle Sage was high and had forgotten her there. They said that it had happened before but my uncle would clean her up and put her to bed before my parents came home from work.

The men on the corner, who stood there with beers in their hand in front of the store, explained to each other what my uncle had told them. They said my uncle said that he would get rock hard whenever he picked her up because her "flower was so fresh and innocent." They would tell each other how he pushed his rock hard stick inside of her, pushing, and pushing, and pushing until her little body was forced opened to accept him. They talked about how my uncle would say he jabbed his rod to the back of her throat until she threw up and made her suck, then did her anally. Nobody knew what to do for her. But for the rest of her life, until Tamalah left, my mother held and squeezed her, never wanting to let her go.

I guess my mother was grieving because in her

mind she had lost her little girl to her brother-in-law. She watched her child die emotionally. But Tamalah was two! I never understood how she relived all of this – she was only two years old. But my mother relived it for the rest of her life, grieving herself to death. There was no escaping.

My sister was home. And there was time, after all, to bond with her. My hopes had subsided when I learned Tamalah was only home to steal some things from the house. After I hugged her, smelling her inborn perfume scent of leaves from a magnolia tree topped with the sweet mellifluous aroma of amber, I gave her my Atari and my school clothes but it wasn't enough for her.

She must have been in trouble with someone! Tamalah was shot and killed that night. She died two nights before my mother transitioned of "natural causes," the doctors said but she died from grief and a broken heart, I say. Tamalah killed my mama.

Two nights before, she was caught climbing out of a window of a bright multi-colored house on Caffin Avenue with a jewelry box. The bullet went into her left shoulder blade and came out of her the right side of her neck. Yeah, daddy my sister is dead, and my mama too!

We sat staring, me, my daddy, and Sage, listening to Triggerman in the cassette player. Soon, they had no love for what was truly beautiful. My daddy and Sage were left docile men, shells of anger waiting to explode soon unable to utilize their own judgment, and hip hop became my parent serving as a bullhorn which echoed the voices of the ancestors.

The US Army Corp of Engineers are asking for billions of dollars, in addition to the billions they have been given already to secure the levees. There is corruption and chaos, but the spirits of the people are genuine. People have gone back to grassroot demonstrations such as marches to fight political attacks. In the midst of existing confusion, survivors who are stranded in other states are being swindled from their right to vote in a mayoral election this month because they are not in Louisiana.

However, soldiers who are displaced in Iraq, under false allegations I might add, have the right to vote by satellite but not residents of New Orleans who are only out of their homes due to one of America's worst natural disasters..

This city has been exposed for its racial biases that have long been a part its history. The media has run with a statement made by the black mayor of New Orleans; but they have swept away the racial statements made by a white political leader and candidate in the race for mayor. Pawpaw always told me to watch the story as it underlines what is not seen or heard. He said I should learn from the underlined story and tell it just as I see it.

New Orleans was destroyed by levees, not Hurricane Katrina. In their knowing, the levee at the Industrial Canal in the Lower Ninth Ward being barged purposely to salvage the French Quarter (tourism industry) is questionable to some but apparent to others. For those who continue to question the allegations, I ask: If the levee breach was due to design failure in the year 2005, why wasn't that design corrected in 1965 after Hurricane Betsy flooded homes in that same area?

I was told by older generations that the levee was barged then as well, for a reason that is unchanged. Yes, they said that! The year 2009 brought on a lawsuit because they are saying it was a runaway barge that destroyed the levee of the Industrial Canal. Whatever the case may be, the levee break was no accident in generational knowing.

By the way, the President of the United States, in 1965, walked the streets of the Ninth Ward and personally delivered meals after Hurricane Betsy to residents who were in Washington Elementary School located on St. Claude Avenue. He was there as the suffering began. In 2005, the Federal Government left American citizens to die. It looks like genocide.

The tourism industry has long awaited land that is owned by blacks. This city's history tells us this land proposed for cruise ship docks was the only land poor black New Orleanians were allowed to purchase. It is the lowest grounds in the city, but it became their homes.

Pawpaw bought a lot on this land. He worked hard all of his life to maintain his property and the property of his neighbors. My grandparents are no longer with us. Their house has collapsed. It is completely off of its foundation and on top of my mother's car that was parked in the driveway.

All of my family's memories were held in that house. We were there on holidays as a family. We were there to communicate as a family. We were there to love the whole family, in that house. My voice will be heard on the behalf of Lulu and Pawpaw. My voice will be heard along with the fight for homes in the Lower Ninth Ward community or whichever way the land will be converted.

My grandparents are owners of real estate property in the Lower Ninth Ward; or, they are owners of a fraction of the potential swamp land below the Industrial Canal. While the decision has yet to be made using flood maps that are issued by the Federal Government and electrical grids that are built by a company hired by the city, residents are without housing. Houses remain in a contaminated state in 2011.

Boogie, my brother, and his girlfriend lived, temporarily, in Houston, Texas. He had been searching for employment, but his appearance screams New Orleans. Boogie is round; he calls it big sexy. His jeans are larger than they have to be and every outfit is accented with a bucket fitting cap with a brim. Not that he goes into business establishments desiring a job dressed that way. But the cap is in his hand when it's not on his head, which isn't often.

He is truly not a briefcase brother. Bruce drove trucks back home, in New Orleans. He delivered liquor to grocery stores and wine cellars. He drove larger trucks before taken that job but never anything that would put him out of immediate contact with Love, or my mama.

Love worked in retail before the storm. The two things she loved most in life, besides Boogie, were stylish clothes and animals. They never heard a word about Fam, their dog. But there is a framed picture of him in their new apartment in Baton Rouge.

Needless to say, both their places of employment were flooded, never rebuilt, and merchandise tarnished. They're working to start over again, again after five years have passed. Houston is where most of New Orleans relocated. But there are many in places like Georgia, Florida, N. Carolina, Maryland, and Arizona. Most New Orleanians are now residents of those states.

My mother's brother was flown to Michigan by rescue crews on the fourth day subsequent to Hurricane Katrina without a way to return. He eventually received assistance from Red Cross and he, now, lives in Phoenix, Arizona. After losing his personal belongings and place of business, he is working to start over.

There are some in places further away like Oregon, California and New York. Though, my mother, Amina and her husband, who is now a friend of mine, are in Plano, Texas. The healthcare system in New Orleans is very close to non-existing, so she cannot come home.

In Texas, nonetheless, she is receiving the medical care she needs. We are grateful. Mama is working to start over. She has never been without Boogie or me, close by. She has never lived alone with her husband. She had never been to Texas and although, she doesn't particularly like it there, she is at peace in her new life.
New life, hmm, takes me back to the story I had been working on...

Lash to back

They roped his neck
They whipped, beat, gore, blood, was castrated
They starve, scorn, was dehumanized
They suffered for my dignity
I am Queen with pride given by them
I am child of Congo Square
I am Africans tainted by the new world
I am wounded, though never was I there
But the hurt is when I can just remember

~~~~~~~~~~~~~~~~~~~~~~~~~~~

We shared stories from back in the day when hip hop was our life. We shared stories expressing what truly was the making of the person standing before me or the making of the person standing before him. We shared recipes, instruments, ideas, and concerns. I shared my heart. And he knew!

I believe he knew of all the guarded love I detained. It was amazing how I expected this man to know what was inside of me. After all, he was just learning me. I was learning him but absorbed more of his soul with each communicable moment. There was a sad place in his soul that I wanted to exuberate. I wanted him to know my wounds. I wanted him to know my insecurities. I wanted him to know my heart; the cut out had been measured and tailored for him.

He is in my dreams.

~~~~~~~~~~~~~~~~~~~~~~~~~~~

Standing in the rain, we were as happy as school aged students at Christmas time. We were just standing there, free with no school, rocking to the best concert ever to hit the streets of New Orleans. Doug E.

Fresh blew up the spot when Slick Rick stepped onto the stage. La-Di-Da-Di is a classic!

Kolunde took my hand and we left backstage to go into the audience front and center like we both did in the old days. In that moment, we had forgotten all of our trivial worries. We were smiling, dancing and rapping as if we were on stage while everyone stood and looked from their shelter in the rain.

When Tiye graduated from Starks University, she became a Professor at The University of Gambia in Banjul. She loved The Gambia. Life for her was fully defined in West Africa. But she would often wonder and even long for her friend Kolunde.

Kolunde now lived in Brooklyn, New York and had given up on concert promotion because he said hip hop was dead. He was found in deep thought two and three times in a day because, to himself, he would whisper "hip hop's not really dead...it's just real cats aren't heard anymore!" "Everybody wanna be a gangsta." His heart couldn't let go of what had kept him sane in his life. "I wanna savor the eclectic threads that were woven to make me who I am, and those threads are the phrases from rhythmic words combined with def melodies that grip hip hop culture."

Ultimately, Kolunde was homesick. Being away from the city always feels like exile for anyone born of New Orleans decent. New Orleans is a country within a country. Its own society of culture bearers who steps outside of life, as the rest of the country knows it, to take a deep breath and live.

Although people worked for a living just as everyone else, which is not believed by the rest of the U.S., they appreciated what was most important. People in New Orleans worked to live, not the other way around.Kolunde, with the soul of an artist, missed his country.

He ended up living in Brooklyn purely by accident. He was called one day, by a West African dance troupe wanting to replace a drummer that had moved back home to Guinea. It was a paying gig that was constant so he decided to go until the company hired another drummer.

What he didn't know was he would be the permanent drummer. Although he didn't mind the work, he wished it had allowed him to remain in New Orleans. But unfortunately for him, all of the shows, for the past three years, were on the northeast coast. As Kolunde played Sorsoner, a traditional West African rhythm, in a show in Newark, he thought of Tiye as she would speak, in bits and pieces, of her reoccurring dream. He remembered her raspy voice and accented dialect…

"The Calinda is the dance I danced in my dream. It is the dance of the ancestors when they celebrated self and invited one another into relationships. I was always adorned with soft, flowing white linen that dragged behind as I stepped forward with a tall beautiful head wrap that shimmered. The air released a romantic scent that hypnotized all that inhaled and you took my hand, in my dream.

We held hands and twirled around on sacred ground as we both inhaled the hypnotic aroma. The sweetest scent nestled the air arousing our wilds as we moved from holding hands to a full embrace. I saw Osun as she moved her mirror toward me to shine my reflection within view.

She then gave me a bouquet to remind me that I am just as charming. We swayed without a smile. I fell in love with you, in my dream. As we swayed, standing on clouds and listening to the African sounds of Alpha Blondy delicately roving through the atmosphere, we smiled. We walked, together, on the edges of paradise, hand in hand, without a word uttered but a soothing vibe that told a million stories.

With your eyes, you told me that I am your wife, as you rubbed your hand along the nap of my neck. And I was quivering inside as I slightly rolled my neck leaning toward what felt so damn good. My hair became exposed and it began to cover my face, but you brushed it away and stared. Still without a word, you moved your hand though my natural tresses with one hand and gently grasped my waist with the other. I slowly moved to the chimes of the melody playing. There we stood on the edge of paradise, wanting, in my dream."

Kolunde realized that he really missed Tiye just as much as he missed New Orleans. He regretted never admitting- that he knew of her love for him. He kept her believing that they were just like childhood friends that were as close as brother and sister. He knew she was in love with him and he let her go. "I wonder if she knew?" Kolunde had been in love with Tiye since the first day he laid eyes on her at Starks. There was a strange vibe about her that intrigued him.

Playing the second half of the show, he remembered when the elevator doors opened and placing his eyes on Tiye as she stood there waiting for him and his friends to get out off of the elevator. He remembered that Tiye acted like she was walking by the elevator and not waiting to go up. He wondered if she was coming to meet the drum beat. He thought, "but she was too late."

Kolunde remembered how startled she looked when the doors opened and how she quickly began walking outside. It was something about her that he, being the curious cat that he was, needed to find. It was her eyes! At the elevator, he remembered, Tiye held her head down avoiding the glances from the other drummers and the piercing stare from him. It was in her eyes!

Her eyes told a story that coincided with his hollowed heart. They told a familiar story tucked underneath a creative backdrop. Her eyes told her life's story. And Kolunde was drawn to her by them.

Mama Enike' was a voluptuously beautiful woman with skin that shined like wet onyx displaying her highlighted differences but paralleled color tones and exquisite bone structure. Her coarse hair was thick and long mahogany that had "never been treated by the chemicals." That's what Kolunde's father would say anyway.

Tiye reminded Kolunde of his mother. She looked more like a younger version of Mama Enike'. Strikingly, Tiye looked just like Tamalah, Kolunde's sister. Tiye had never laid eyes on Tamalah but somehow she moved and smelled like the two women Kolunde loved more than anything in his life, including hip hop.

Enike's youngest child had vowed to never end up like Big Alyji. He promised the great ruler of his head that he would never become an angry, maimed creature who could never see past the pain in which he harbored. Kolunde held tight to his elekes. He wore those sacred beads around his neck to protect and guarantee that he would live and keep the promise he had made to himself.

The necklaces, one made of six red beads patterned with six white beads and the other with seven alternating white and blue beads, was indeed the protection that guaranteed his safety according to his faith. Ifa had become the ground in which Tiye and Kolunde stood firmly upon since their teen years.

Kolunde would often fly down from New York to visit Big Alyji in New Orleans, if not for anything else but to make sure he was eating properly. He would always stop to pick up fruits to bring with him like papayas, watermelon and routinely, a blue and white plate filled with fried plantains.

He would also visit the places he and Tiye frequented. The Claiborne Bridge, to him, lost all of its exuberance now that the "Dope is Death" banner was gone. But he soon noticed the old guy, who had seemed to be an old man all of Kolunde's life. He was still seated under the bridge with his boom box covered with a handmade tin can shield securing what was his livelihood still blasting oldies but goodies, usually Ernie K. Doe.

He had the speakers Kolunde remembered his daddy having when he was two years old. He felt the warmth of being home. Kolunde would walk under the oak trees that aligned Esplanade Avenue to City Park and sit near the carousal. He remembered blissfully floating upward then downward on the white horse that Tiye loved so much. He reminisced about the day when Tiye tumbled backward in the playground area, when it was quite difficult to distinguish the grown-ups from the children, playing on the swings with a quick chuckle to his self. "I rather reminisce over you, my God," he mumbled as he headed back to his car, on foot down, Esplanade Avenue.

My family was at their witts end the year my cousin died. We all traveled to Michigan to comfort and console his mother. Kolunde came with us which was not surprising because he was a part of the Burgundi/Mercadel family. He loved my cousin just as much as I did.

I told him that Jacques was diagnosed with cancer the day I found out. It would have certainly been beneficial to be a fly on the wall the day Kolunde visited Jacques. Whatever was said, Aunt Rose said, "Jacques was without worry after he left." She said his face was illuminated with life as if he had just recognized it still filled his lungs with every breath he was able to take. He was as calm as the breeze, no longer frightened of his illness. I'm not surprised though. My Kolunde was an emotional healer to all people.

As I sat on Kairaba Avenue at The Café, a restaurant in Serekunda with my new family, I would drift away. Ade, my husband, always challenged "a penny for your thoughts?" He was a kind man, very educated and well raised by his mother. I would always drift back to the life I led in the States and mentally compare the wounded brothers there to the ancestral loving men here in The Gambia. And my God, were they beautiful!

To me, they all belonged in a museum as sculptured pieces of art. Gees! I had only known men in The United States as wounded or angry. Although I know better. But my judgment always led me to the wrong man.

I felt Kolunde's hand in mine and heard his baritone voice in my head as a murmur: "make sure you choose a man who is passionate about more than only you in his life, It is then when he will know to love you."

Ade was a teacher. He taught at Ndows Comprehensive School in Fajara, a suburb in The Gambia. It was amazing to watch him work with the students. They were receptive to every integrated studies lesson Mr. Campell set before them. They loved him and I did too – for what he provided me.

Tall, deep chocolate brown skinned, large, muscular build, nearly natted, wise, gentle man – I fell I love with him
He is my love – never made music. I didn't want too until one year…
Sweaty passion
Sticky love muscles
Soft tongue caresses sang crescendo tones
After time, winds had blown I wondered what did I do
I really did love him. I praised his majesty. I longed for the wisdom words that dripped from his tongue as we mentally sat on the shores of Niger River Delta and listened to the ancestors sing.
My skin dampened at his every diminutive touch but the time held too much when his secret was revealed
Time held too much when I, too, had the same new secret
Two men- I loved them both – for different reasons and if combining them was an option, I would have the perfect husband
but what about him?
Will his wife understand this elongated relationship on the outer surface of matrimony – that lady's husband forever linger around my spirit,
in the spirit
That lady's husband – Tall, deep chocolate brown skinned, large muscular build, nearly natted, wise, gentle man – I fell in love with him
He is my love

Twilight night shade of skin, broad shoulders, smooth cut hair, rough man's man, passionate beautiful spirited man – I fell in love with him
He is my foundation, my support, my King that cherished my soul
I felt his warm cares. I seized his nourishment. I tasted his love in the core of my being. I am safe. And time held too much when I married him.
Tall, twilight night deep chocolate brown shade of skin, large hands, nearly natted, strong, muscular build, broad shoulders, rough man's man, powerful, passionate, wise provider, gentleman,
beautiful spirited man
They are my loves.

Chapter Twelve

Looking Back

I have encountered many obstacles in my life. The aftermath of Hurricane Katrina has proven to be the whammy. I believe survival is about movement. New Orleans is full of movers, and the city will survive. I, and my family (the members that are left), will survive. I have no job because the independent African centered educational facility of which I taught Language Arts received over 50% flood damage.

In 2006, I had no home because the house that I bought three years prior was filled to the ceiling with waters from the Mississippi River by way of the Industrial Canal. Even though it has gotten me out of harm's way and back, my little Cavalier died; so soon I will have no car. And once again, I am starting over again and will succeed. But it has dawned on me that I have a story to tell. It is held in the pages of my journal. A possibility of becoming a writer is more apparent. I have rebuilt my house to a standard that is livable. And my cavalier has been replaced with a Ford F150.

Currently, I am doctoral student studying Fine Arts without a clue of where tuition money comes from. For that matter, I am even without a clue of where money comes to feed my children, but I am protected by my ancestors so my feet are guided. It was that determination that was instilled in me as a young girl sitting at my grandfather's feet while he smoked a cigar and told stories.

Faith tells us no matter what's in our path, we have to make the next step. As an ordinary woman, born and raised in New Orleans and faced with personal barriers daily, that is how I have lived my life. This is what will carry us through. It doesn't occur to happen any other way. All is not well! There is major work to do! But I'd like to say to the world, we are not broken.

Nice try Katrina!

Aunt Rose wrote a letter to me last year telling me about the goings on in New Orleans. She told me how the politics were screwed up as usual and that she had moved from Michigan and bought a house in my old neighborhood, Treme. She told me that she ran into Kolunde and his wife at the International Festival in Marconi Meadows.

His wife…I thought to myself. I don't know how the letter read after that sentence. I never mustered up the courage to read it to the end. I was so afraid that the letter was going to say that he had children with this woman, the children whose names I carried in my heart until they existed. And who was this woman? Where did she come from? Why didn't I know of her?

As I dried my tears, I quickly went to the phone booth on the corner of the compound where I lived and attempted to call Kolunde. Needless to say, the number had been changed and I was unable to reach him. Maybe he didn't love me after all. I have waited all of my life to love him outside of my own mind. I've tried to call him from the same booth for the past year without success.

I married him. Ade Campell. I married him and became Mrs. Tiye Campell, reluctantly. He loved me. I respected him.

~~~~~~~~~~~~~~~~~~~~~~~~~~~

"Ade, I have to go home." I just couldn't take it any longer. "Ade, I have to go home," is what I said right after he came. I'm sorry but I have to go. As Ade lied there breathing hard with sweat trickling from his brow, I quickly got up, covered my mouth as if I was holding back vomit with my hand and ran to shower. What I was holding was the sound of my soul's thunderous cry shouting out "KOLUNDE!!!!."

"Ade, I have to go home." I just couldn't take it any longer. "Ade, I have to go home," is what I said right after he came. I'm sorry, but I have to go. As Ade lied there breathing hard with sweat trickling from his brow, I quickly got up, covered my mouth as if I was holding back vomit with my hand and ran to shower. What I was holding was the sound of my soul's thunderous cry shouting out "ALIJI KOLUNDE!!!!."

Ade followed, "Tiye are you alright? Tiye, you're scaring me! Are you okay!" "Yes, I am Ade, very softly and sympathetically, Tiye whispered. "I must go now." "Go where?" Ade was puzzled. "I am leaving to go home, Ade. Although I am grateful to have met you, I must return to my life in New Orleans for now."

"How long will you be there, Tiye? You are my wife," Ade shouted because in the back of his mind he knew Tiye was returning to her one true love. Ade had been aware of Tiye's heart from the beginning. She told her

story with her eyes whenever he made love to her. Ade knew, but did Kolunde?

Tiye didn't even pack her things. After stepping out of the shower, she immediately wrapped two yards of material around her and slipped her feet into a pair of handmade leather flip flops that were sold on the corner, down the street in the market. She rushed to the top dresser drawer to grab a mudcloth handbag that carried all of her important papers and left Ade standing there in amazement, naked and baffled.

At that moment, Ade confusion transitioned to rage. He thought to himself, "I'm gonna kill her!" He began throwing oak carved furniture around the bedroom as if they were made of cardboard as he looked for his underpants or any pants. He was going to get her! Never in a woman's life can she just up and leave her husband. "I have a very authoritative name here in The Gambia. Who does she think she is?"

Ade ran after Tiye with her wrapper around his waist. No shoes. No shirt. No underpants. He ran out with Tiye's wrapper around his waist and fury on his face. Luckily for Tiye, she'd hopped into a bush taxi that just so happen to be passing as she walked out to the highway. The driver, after dropping off all of his other passengers, transported her from her safe haven with a man whom genuinely loved her to the arctic and bustling scene at the airport in Dakar, Senegal.

Tiye was crying when she boarded with the driver. He wondered if her husband had beaten her. He wondered if her children had gone away. He wondered if her husband had decided to take another wife because she did not bore a man child. He wondered and the only reason he drove her to the neighboring country through the tumultuous dirt roads in the pouring rain was due to sheer nosiness. The streets of the land are full of gossip.

"You going to Ole Skool in the Park with us?" Auntie Rose was glad to see that I was home from Africa. She understood nothing about Africa. She only knew what almost all of the traditionally raised African Americans knew. It was far. They don't like us. Oh, and "I don't wanna go there because they are poor and have AIDS."

It was truly a different world, a different scent, a totally different vibe when I got off of the plane at Louis Armstrong International Airport. What a feeling! It was hard to accept that this is the place in which I was born. It was even harder to have thrown back in my face that I, too, was one of those African Americans who never wanted to go to Africa. But that was a long time ago.

I remember my mama telling me that "those women are animals" as she described the pain of child birth. "They pop out the baby and move around like nothing ever happened to them!" My goodness, there is so much buried in my subconscious. Anyway, with a sigh of relief from the feeling of Auntie Rose's warm embrace, I said, yeah, I'm coming to the park. I was really hoping to see Kolunde, didn't know much about his whereabouts. All I knew was the old spots we hung out in when we were younger.

Leaning on the concrete lion in the park, I begin tapping my feet to "a cleanup woman is a woman who *takes all the love we girls leave behind." In the middle of my finger snap all the clouds in the sky weighed heavily on my shoulders like bricks. Where is Kolunde? Who is this woman? Will I ever see him again? These three questions played forward and backwards, backwards and forward in my head, as if someone was hitting the play button on a recorder, and evilly, pressing rewind to play it over and over and over again.*

Then they came. There they were. Tears were rolling down my face, and I couldn't control them. Where is my Kolunde? I cried like no one was there. My legs became weak; I slumped to the ground. His wife! Who the hell is his wife?

Self-pity and pain quickly transitioned to anger. AAAAHHHHH! AAAAAHHHHH! I began screaming at the top of my lungs, they say. "It's alright, baby," Auntie Rose said as she gently caressed my forehead. "Now, I think it's time for you to tell Auntie what's going on." "You know we love you but I can't help you when I don't know what's wrong." I opened my eyes just a little wider to see where I was…in…in a hospital. WHAT THE HELL!

"No!" "Wait!" "Wait! Tiye!" "Baby, please come back." Consciously, I could hear Aunt Rose calling me but my feet were moving, my heart was racing. I couldn't stop running until it was black. I couldn't see nothing! I only heard a loud noise then I was flat on my back with a blood covered face. "I'm sorry, Mrs. Mercadel," we're going to have to keep Tiye in our facility for closer observation. The incident this evening was a bit nasty. She has broken her nose. And her heart rate is slightly abnormal at this time. We are doing everything we can

to assist her in regaining consciousness, and we believe she will be alright. "Can I see her." "She's in ICU at this time because of her heart condition so there's a limitation on visitors, but I'll come out to get you in just a few minutes."

Note to self - Remember to finish...Potential title: Let Me Taste

Mayor Ray Nagin speaking to residents at a rally before the march held on April 1, 2006 in New Orleans. Residents and supporters across the nation marched over the GNO Bridge (The Greater New Orleans Bridge runs across the Mississippi River connecting the downtown business district of Orleans parish to Jefferson parish). This demonstration was to unite the masses in order to have one voice to speak out against discrimination, unfair elections, and public education. Also, the march was to memorialize the would be evacuees who were stranded for days in the flood waters after Hurricane Katrina. Although starving and soiled, they were turned back by armed deputies to their demise, seemingly

The march, led by Rev. Jessie Jackson, was supported by such leading figures as Al Sharpton, Judge Mathis, Bill Cosby, John Legend and many other black political and social leaders. They were alongside local leading figures of New Orleans like William Jefferson, Cedric Richmond, Former Mayor Marc Morial and many, many, more. All mixed in with the residents (all races) of New Orleans and various cities for one cause

And still residents were united with all cultures and races in the city of New Orleans working for progression in 2009.

Cybernetics & Paradoxes

The Author's Commentary

Family Synchronization

There are many shifts in perspective leadership within family structural paradigm. Most times, during these shifts, the family system suffers a traumatic grief. "The behavior of every individual within the family is related to and dependent upon the behavior of all the others. (Watzlawick, 1967, pp.134)" But, if there is a long existing framework that describes the attributes and ways of knowing of a family that has suddenly been destroyed, or consciously shifted in structure, the individual pragmatics become foreign.

  This story was written to recursively display such shifts. The Burgundi family was initially patriarchial; Mr. Walter Burgundi, Sr. was the leader. Burgundi's death conferred tumultuous undercurrents when the family became matriarchal through his granddaughter whom he had groomed to lead. Karasi carried out the cycle from which her grandfather traveled in his leadership path.

  Although she wondered (oftentimes rebelled) from where her strength and determination would come, it did not stop her. She worked to build a new format for communication in her family. "As a broken winged bird," though, she was internally suffering with her own freedom to communicate effectively with her children, especially Tia. This is a cybernetically charged behavior, or a behavior that has been accepted in relationship but suggests a circular way of relating provided by generational knowing (i.e. relations/communication between Amina, Karasi and Tia, perhaps beginning with Lulu).

In Pragmatics of Human Communications, Watzlawick, et al. talks about actions that are taken or statements that are made for unknown or inexplicable reasons. He claims, "We are constantly in communication, and yet we are almost completely unable to communicate about communication. (p. 36)" I am defining communication as being the comprehension and wisdom transferred in dialogue and presence among lived paradoxes in collective settings. In this particular family's routine operations, it became a case of cybernetics of cybernetics, second order cybernetics, the circularity of an existing cycle of nonverbal communication, tucked away visceral emotions, and pain while working to reach a combined goal. That combined goal was to carry Mr. Burgundi's vision for growth and unity within the family system.

Laced Bloodline is a book of empowerment for formative minds in later years. It tells of a life filled with struggle and the successful outcome. It teaches how one should always, in the midst of mental or physical battle, sustain a positive way of thinking.

In the early years, adulthood is an orb of confusion; and with proper guidance mistakes can be avoided or cushioned to make future goals attainable without delay. As the storyline is laced with music lyrics, an allusion to African-American history, and humor, the reading of this book is sure to capture the attention of young adults/teens keeping them eager to read literature in a cyber society.

Simulated Lesson Plan

The following illustrates a simulated lesson plan for Laced Bloodline which gives opportunity for learning through critical discussion, not authoritative teaching.

Day 1: The class will have open discussion on the lives destroyed by Hurricane Katrina or any other disaster. Students will share their thoughts about the natural disasters and the people it affected. Were all people affected by the hurricane?

Why did the levees fail to keep the Mississippi River out of New Orleans? Why were residents fighting to return to their homes in a city in great need of rebuilding an entire infrastructure? The students will read "The Gumbo

Bowl," after discussion, making mental notes of the chapter. Afterward the class is open to discuss the reading assignment.

60 minutes
Rubric: 20 minute discussion
20 minute reading
20 minute discussion

Day 2: Students are given the opportunity to recap the previous discussion and reading. This will allow students to recapture the interest and/or concern from the preceding class period. How and where does the story begin? Who is the narrator? Why do you think the initial chapter is called "The Gumbo Bowl?" The students will read the next two chapters, after discussion, making mental notes. Afterward, the class is open to discuss the reading assignment.

60 minutes
Rubric: 20 minute discussion
20 minute reading
20 minute discussion

Day 3: Students are given the opportunity to recap previous discussion and reading. This will allow students to identify with the characters pulled from "The Gumbo Bowl." What do you think about Valentin Castillo? This discussion allows questions and/or comments about people from other countries. Mr. Castillo also opens the students imagination and awareness about people all over the world who are of African descent. Students will discuss culture and history. This discussion will teach the importance of understanding Africans relocated through the diaspora. Who is Bruce Thibodeaux? Why do you think fatigue trounced Bruce early Sunday morning? What kind of relationship does Bruce have with his sister? If you had to describe his appearance, what would be the most descriptive attributes?

Students will read the next two chapters. The classroom is open for a 10 minute discussion to allow students to digest the assigned reading.

60 minutes
Rubric: 20 minute discussion
20 minute reading
20 minute discussion

Day 4: Students are given the opportunity to recap previous discussion and reading. How much has Trey absorbed in his short life? Is Valentin important to Trey? Why or why not? Where does Nelson fit in Trey's life? How do you think Tia Burgundi has taken this drastic change in her routine life? Do you think she was a happy girl before the evacuation? Why or why not? What kind of things have affected her life so far? What kind of issues these children may possibly face in the future?

How will they overcome their potential issues? Students will read the next two chapters silently. Was Karasi reared similar to the way she raises Tia? Do you think the unhappy childhood became a cycle in this family?

1hour, 15 minutes
Rubric: 10 minute discussion
25 minute discussion
20 reading
20 minute discussion

Day 5: Students are given the opportunity to recap previous discussion and reading. One student will have the opportunity to read a poem from "In my journal" aloud. After reading is complete, one student will give an explanation of the poem that was read. Students will read "The Gumbo Bowl" silently. The classroom will be open to discuss the outcome of Hurricane Katrina. What are the remaining issues facing the city of New Orleans? How has Pawpaw empowered Karasi? What role does determination play in your life? Why is movement important in life?

1 hour, 15 minutes
Rubric: 10 minute discussion
30 minute poetry reading and discussion

20 minute reading
15 minute discussion on the important of movement in life

Subject:
- English
- Social Justice
- Life Skills/Leadership Awareness
- Cultural Anthropology
- Creative Writing

Grade Level:
High school seniors or college freshmen and beyond

Content: Content will consist of a real life story, day-to-day relations encountered by the reading of Laced Bloodline. There is no explicit material but the subject matter is not appropriate for younger readers who have not yet been exposed to instances which requires adult decision making.

Objective: The student will learn critical thinking as they strengthen reading skills. They will be exposed to skills needed for coping with the hardships of life. The students will also learn to interact with each other promoting useful dialog about life.

Procedure: Provoke controlled critical dialog in the classroom increasing the severity of the subject matter. Assign reading of chapters while in the classroom observing the students as they read.

Materials:
- Laced Bloodline
- Black Board

- Journals
- Writing tools

Assessments: Make certain each student participates in the discussions using the critical pedagogy and linguistic exchange method. Have students record their comments, ideas, and questions in their journals. Ask that they share their comments and questions with the class for further discussion about movement in life.

Critical Pedagogy – *a theory of teaching used to assist students with traveling down a road filled with thought provoking ideals to gain critical consciousness. When this line of reasoning is at its peak, students are encouraged to share this knowledge and attempt to solve the social issues that have been viewed as oppressive through discussion.*

Follow-up Activities: In-class journal readings with life matters, or potential life matters being the topic of each entry.

References

Banks-Wallace, JoAnne. (2006). Talk that Talk: Storytelling and Analysis Rooted in African American Oral Tradition, Columbia: Qualitative Health Research Journal Vol. 12

Bateson, Gregory. (1956). Toward a Theory of Schizophrenia. Behavioral Science Vol.1, Issue 4, pp. 251-264

Behar, Ruth. (1996). The Valuable Observer: anthropology that breaks your heart. Boston: Beacon Press

Bloomquist, J., (2009). Class and Categories: What role does socioeconomic status plays in Children's Lexical and Conceptual Development? Multilingua: Journal of Cross-Cultural and Interlanguage Communication. Vol. 28, Issue 4, Abstract

Bloomquist, J. (2009). The Science of Language. Gettysburg Faculty Authors Series, interview

Bloomquist, J. (2003). Cross-Cultural Semantic Acquisition: Evidence from over-extentions in child language. Dissertation, University at Buffalo

Freire, P., Shor, I. (1987). A Pedagogy for Liberation Dialouges on Transforming Education. New York: Bergin & Garvey

Hammond, Evelyn. (2003). The Logic of Difference: A History of Race in Science and of Afro American Studies. San Francisco: California Newsreel

Irele, A., Jeyifo, B. (2010). The Oxford Encyclopedia of African Thought Vol. 1. New York: Oxford University Press

Jost, J. Kay, A., Thorisdottir, H. (2009). Social and Psychological bases of Ideology and System Justification. New York: Oxford University Press

Karenga, M. (2006). The Rhetoric of Race: towards a revolutionary construction of black identity. Valencia: University of Valencia

Keeney, Bradford., (1983). Aesthetics of Change. New York: The Guilford Press

Morin, E. (1996). A New Way of Thinking –The Art of Complexity Issue 2. Paris: UNESCO Courier February

Morin, Edgar. (2008). On Complexity. New Jersey: Hampton Press Inc.

Smith, K., Berg, D. (1987). Paradoxes of Group Life Understanding Conflict, Paralysis, and Movement in Group Dynamics. San Francisco: John Wiley & Sons, Inc.
Stewart, E., Bennett, M. (1991). American Cultural Patterns: A Cross-Cultural Perspective. Boston: Intercultural Press.

Watzlawick, P., Bevelas, J., Jackson, D. (1967). Pragmatics of Human Communication. A Study of Interactional Patterns, Pathologies, and Paradoxes. New York: W. W. Norton & Company

Wilson, Amos. (1991). Awakening the Natural Genuis of Black Children. New York: Afrikan World InfoSystems

About the Author

[Double Click To Add Text]